INSIDE FANTASY FOOTBALL

INSIDE FANTASY FOOTBALL

America's Favorite Non-Contact Sport

PETER FUNT

Jefferson Bay Books

Copyright © 2024 by Peter Funt

All rights reserved.

Published by Jefferson Bay Books.
No portion of this book may be reproduced, stored in a retrieval system or transmitted in any form or by any means, mechanical, electronic, photocopying, recording or otherwise, without written permission.

Hardcover ISBN: 978-1-7376267-6-3
Paperback ISBN: 978-1-7376267-5-6

Printed in the United States

First Edition: August 2024

Please direct inquiries regarding excerpts from this book, video clips or interviews to: Media@CandidCamera.com

ABOUT THE COVER

We counted the number of YouTube channels devoted to fantasy football. Anyone taking the "under" on, say, 250, would have been wiped out. The answer was 600+.

Several of the popular channels are pictured on the cover including:

- Legendary Upside
- Establish the Run
- Fantasy Life
- Underdog Fantasy
- Liam Murphy
- Peter Overzet's Deposit Kingdom
- NFL on NBC Fantasy Football Happy Hour
- FantasyPros

Thanks to them all.

DEDICATION

In doing my interviews for this project, the comment I heard most was, "I learned about fantasy football from my dad." Though my son Danny did learn a lot about sports from me, I first played fantasy football thanks to him. For that alone he gets this dedication. But there's plenty more: Danny is a top notch journalist and his book about sports gambling, due in 2025, is sure to be a hit. Plus, he's an all-around good guy.

CONTENTS

Foreword..15

1 / Fantasy Football's Reality
50+ million players and billions of dollars........................19

2 / Fun and Games
Parlor Foot-ball sets the course..................................33

3 / They Called it "GOPPPL"
Wink's basement hosts the first draft............................47

4 / A Whole New Ballgame
Fantasy goes to print and digital................................63

5 / The Daily Difference
DFS puts a new $pin on fantasy games............................79

6 / Major Media Get Hooked
Networks and the NFL are all in.................................97

7 / Best Ball...Mania
All play and no work...109

8 / Top Talking Touts
Talk is cheap — and there's plenty of it.......................125

9 / The Players' Perspective
They're either all in or all out..*151*

10 / Celebrities Huddle Up
Hooray for Hollywood..*161*

11 / The Richest 2 Percent
Fantasy football has made many millionaires.....................*175*

12 / Leagues of Their Own
Women are a growing fantasy force....................................*193*

13 / Techno Touchdowns
Is AI changing fantasy forever?..*209*

Appendix
Fantasy football terminology..*223*

Index..*240*

*"Thank you, fantasy football draft,
for letting me know that even in my fantasies
I am bad at sports."*
—*Jimmy Fallon*

FOREWORD

ON A RAINY OCTOBER SUNDAY I was holed up in a room at Kennedy Airport's TWA Hotel, prior to attending my niece Katie's wedding. A knock at the door signaled the arrival of my nephews, Jake, Alex and Nick, who found me with my feet up, watching the 49ers game on the large wall-mounted TV. Two other NFL games were running on my laptop via Sunday Ticket, and I was using my iPhone for player updates from Yahoo and ESPN. Though the three teens had a rudimentary knowledge of pro football, I was taken aback when they revealed that unlike me and some 50 million other Americans they had never learned about the fantasy version — a burgeoning billion-dollar enterprise.

As I launched into a crash course about the game, I was struck by the serendipity of the moment. It was on a similarly rain-soaked weekend in 1962, in this same TWA terminal building, that Bill Winkenbach, a minority owner of the positively awful Oakland Raiders, flew in for a Sunday game against the Titans (later the Jets). Depressed over his team's dismal record and lack of promotable stars, he and some colleagues spent hours inventing a competition that would allow them to roster players from every professional team — at least on paper. It was the birth of fantasy football.

For me and the boys, two pleasing developments occurred that day (in addition to attending Katie and Garrett's beautiful wedding ceremony). We formed The TWA Hotel League, using Yahoo's platform for a weekly four-team fantasy competition. Moreover, I decided to take a deep dive into fantasy football research in order to write this book.

Over the years I had become increasingly immersed in fantasy football — obsessed at times, perhaps, but certainly not addicted, which is an important distinction. I've never spent (or won) much money. I might invest a few hundred dollars each year on season-long and daily contests; some years I turn a small profit, in others I'm wiped out. Either way, it gradually evolved that the fantasy game became more important to me than the real competition on the field — which is exactly how the NFL and its media partners prefer it. We'll poke around to examine that matter in the chapters to follow.

As a kid I engaged in what could loosely be called fantasy sports without ever using the term to describe it. I spent hours holding a bat in front of a mirror, fantasizing that I was Mickey Mantle. In the fall I'd run routes in the backyard, with my pal Ray Mendelsohn lofting spirals as I pretended to be Frank Gifford making the grabs. It wasn't until many years later that my son Danny and his friend Ryan became hooked on fantasy football in Yahoo public leagues and they persuaded me to give it a try. Soon I became curious about the motivation folks have for playing fantasy sports ... the increasingly diverse forms the games have taken ... the growing universe of fantasy touts and experts ... the relationship between the NFL and the fantasy world ... the unmistakable links with sports gambling ... and the mushrooming impact of technology and AI on fantasy competition.

My goal for this book was to probe those topics and others, but not to offer a how-to guide for winning. There are dozens of such books and hundreds of videos devoted to strategy — most created by people better suited to the task than I. (That said, if you sample such stuff you'll discover an abundance of pseudo advice being peddled by people who are probably no more skilled at figuring out draft picks or making weekly start/sit decisions than the rest of us.)

If you're new to fantasy football you might want to check the appendix that covers basics in the form of a glossary.

As for The TWA Hotel League, I warned my nephews the first day that I'm what Yahoo calls a "veteran," devoting many hours each week to studying stats, gathering tidbits from local beat reporters, and digesting advice from people like NBC's Matthew Berry, ESPN's Field Yates, and Al Zeidenfeld, who won a million dollars in 2016 and parlayed it into a touting empire on YouTube and ESPN. The boys were duly impressed with my savvy until our first week's results were posted. Alex scored a solid 151 points. Nick had 132. Jake totaled 126. And I was thoroughly humiliated with 67.

Though I did manage to finish the season in first place — and actually had decent results in my other leagues — it was a vivid reminder that luck plays a big part in this devilish competition. As the legendary Redskins' quarterback Joe Theismann once explained, "Nobody in football should be called a genius. A genius is a guy like Norman Einstein."

Peter Funt
Pebble Beach, California

CHAPTER 1

Fantasy Football's Reality

*Drafters are on the clock
at the Fantasy Football Expo in Canton, Ohio.*

It was 3 a.m. and Will Hsu, 45, a ginseng farmer in central Wisconsin about 100 miles west of Green Bay, couldn't sleep. Nothing unusual about that — especially on Sundays during football season. A dedicated fantasy football player and Packers fan, Hsu had multiple lineups for NFL games spinning in his head. He sent a few WeChat messages to acquaintances in China and wondered how his favorite player, receiver Davante Adams, might do later that day on the road against the Baltimore Ravens. As things turned out, Adams scored a touchdown, making Hsu happy. But it took the other players in Hsu's lineup to make him rich.

An estimated 50 million Americans play fantasy football, and on December 19, 2021 Hsu was among 180,000 of them competing in the DraftKings contest known as Milly Maker, offering a dreamworthy million-dollar prize. Reflecting the strength of its grip on pro football, DraftKings markets itself as the "Official Daily Fantasy Partner of the NFL."

There are essentially two types of fantasy football: seasonal and daily. The seasonal game usually involves drafting a roster and managing it throughout the full NFL season in a league with typically no more than a dozen participants ("best ball" has emerged as a popular alternate form of seasonal play, more about which later). On the other hand, in daily fantasy sports (DFS) a roster is selected each week, most commonly with a budget system in which the best real-life players have the highest salaries. The daily competition could be among dozens of people or thousands, and serious DFS players like Will Hsu invest in multiple entries.

A Harvard MBA, Hsu was never much of an athlete but he had a great mind for statistics. "I started playing fantasy sports in college during the late 1990s as fantasy football transitioned from newspapers to online," he says. "I got into DFS after I moved home to Wisconsin to take over the family business in 2011. A lot of my friends I played season-long fantasy sports with started getting married and having kids. A few of my friends turned to DFS with small invite-only contests on the DraftKings platform for our friend group that played season-long. It was actually a brilliant move because we can choose to play or not play in any given week or contest and not have to worry about coordinating a draft time, not getting a player you really want on your team, people losing interest halfway through the season, collecting and distributing money, etc."

As he watched the Packers-Ravens game on TV that memorable December afternoon, a late touchdown by Baltimore quarterback Tyler Huntley brought the Ravens to within one point of the Packers, 31-30, and Hsu tantalizingly close to a life-changing win. However, a tie and resulting overtime could quite possibly mess things up because thousands of other fantasy players would get bonus playing time to add points. When Ravens coach Jim Harbaugh went for the win by attempting a two-point conversion, Hsu felt elated because no matter what happened next the game would not go into overtime.

He tweeted:

It ended perfectly for me, attempt to Andrews from Huntley. Either way complete or not I should be fine. Just no Def return for a Conversion. XP and OT then all bets are off as someone from the field could still win. So thanks to the @Ravens for going for 2!

The two-point conversion attempt failed.

A short while later, Hsu received a text from DraftKings with official news on how his $45 investment had fared:

Congrats wphsu99, you won a DraftKings 2021-2022 Tournament of Champions entry. Your ticket expires in 365 days.

Then, this message:

You have won $1,185,759.45!

"It was like watching a winning Lotto drawing live," Hsu said. "You don't quite believe it, is that real?" So he and his family celebrated becoming instant millionaires in the only way they could think of. They watched "The Sound of Music" on TV.

◆ ◆ ◆

Since its birth in the 1960s fantasy football has grown into an $11 billion business for providers such as ESPN, DraftKings, FanDuel and Yahoo, as well as the NFL itself. DraftKings and FanDuel alone pay out a combined total of over $2 billion in fantasy winnings each season. It's become such an integral part of the NFL's success formula that, by rule, all NFL stadiums must display fantasy football stats for spectators.

After years of being ignored, and then ridiculed by both NFL owners and players, fantasy football is today fully embraced and promoted. For TV networks and advertisers fantasy football is the perfect "glue," holding fans' interest during even the most lopsided games. Though fantasy competition is based on actual performances on the field, it operates in a way that is fundamentally different from real life. In fantasy sports, allegiance to teams means nothing; individual players are all that matter. In most fantasy football formats each participant creates a roster by selecting individual players from among the NFL's 32 real teams. So, your quarterback might be from the Kansas City Chiefs, while your wide receiver is from the Dallas Cowboys. Your score is based on how well each of your players performs in real games.

The NFL loves this approach so much that most teams actively support, and even invest in, companies that operate fantasy games. Why? Because franchises become more financially stable and fans are more engaged. Nowadays, the sum of the players is greater than the sum of the teams. Moreover, many fantasy players bet with their hearts as well as their wallets.

Any examination of fantasy football must take stock of the two main paths the contests have taken. Their common names are "seasonal" and "daily," but even those terms are imprecise. Seasonal play, which started in 1963, essentially involves a competition extending for all or most of each NFL season — anywhere from 15 to 18 weeks. Daily fantasy sports (DFS), first played a few decades later, refers to competing for a single week of the season or just one day, usually Sunday. But that is only part of what distinguishes the two approaches. In most seasonal contests you are playing in a league, typically consisting of 10 or 12 participants, where NFL players are selected in a draft, and within the league a player is "owned" by just one manager.

In most DFS contests, you are competing with any number of other players, often many thousand. Rather than being drafted, the NFL players are taken according to a salary system which attaches a pretend dollar value to each player based on his skill and likely fantasy value, so a given player can be owned by many managers.

In summary:

Seasonal fantasy allows you to draft a roster of NFL players to be retained throughout the season — unless modified by trades, injuries or waiver claims, according to league rules. The league typically has no more than a dozen participants, who may be friends and colleagues or, alternatively, strangers brought together by an online platform such as Yahoo or ESPN that keeps track of rosters, stats and point totals throughout the season.

Daily fantasy allows you to construct a roster of NFL players for each week's action, based on salaries that relate to players' values. The contests are administered by platforms such as DraftKings and FanDuel and offer prizes of as much as a million dollars or more for the biggest contests.

When critics link fantasy sports to addictive forms of sports betting they are usually referring to DFS. Games that allow multiple entries, feature big money payouts and relaunch daily do, indeed, often mimic elements of conventional gambling.

♦ ♦ ♦

It's easy to quantify the enormous surge in the NFL's popularity. For instance, across all of television — not just sports TV but all TV — 93 of the 100 most-viewed telecasts in 2023 were NFL games. Super Bowl LVIII, in the gambling mecca Las Vegas, was the most-watched television event in U.S. history, according to Nielsen figures, with 123.4 million viewers via CBS, Univision and streaming platforms. A 30-second commercial cost $7 million, up from roughly $4.4 million in 2016 and $37,500 for Super Bowl I back in 1967. With deals spread across multiple outlets — CBS, NBC, Fox, ABC/ESPN, Amazon, Peacock, Netflix and YouTube — the NFL's annual take from TV rights climbed to $11.46 billion in 2024. Over the next decade, the NFL is guaranteed $125.5 billion in television money.

The NFL's 32 teams are valued at an average of $5.1 billion each. In 1960, Lamar Hunt paid $25,000 for the Kansas City Chiefs and today the club is worth $4.3 billion — and that's at the bottom of the rankings. The Dallas Cowboys top the list, with a $9 billion valuation.

Each of the league's 32 teams received just over $400 million following the 2023 season as their share of the NFL pot — an increase of 115 percent in the last decade. The payout does not include ticket sales, local sponsorships, concession sales, etc. (Teams contribute 34 percent of all ticket revenue to an equally shared pool, which is worth another $20 million for each team.)

In 2015, in response to mounting criticism for its outsized revenue flow, the NFL gave up its tax-exempt status, held since 1942. The league now exists as a trade association made up of, and financed by, its 32 member teams. Thirty-one of these teams are owned individually, with the Green Bay Packers organization retaining its nonprofit status. (The Packers have been a publicly-owned, non-profit corporation since 1923. The corporation has some 537,460 stockholders who collectively own an estimated 5.2 million shares of stock following the sixth stock sale in franchise history that took place in 2021.)

The NFL's commissioner, Roger Goodell, has forecast $27 billion in annual revenue for the league by 2027.

One thing that hasn't changed much over the years is attendance at games. On average, NFL stadiums seat about 70,000 people, and for decades the games have usually sold out. What has changed is the ticket price, with the average NFL ticket currently estimated to cost about $151. Even naming stadiums has become lucrative. According to the *Sports Business Journal*, naming rights to So-Fi Stadium in Los Angeles has an annual worth of $30 million while Allegiant Stadium in Las Vegas stands at roughly $25 million per year.

In 2005 the NFL expanded its footprint outside the U.S.,

So-Fi Stadium, opened in 2023, has a $30 million name.

beginning with a game between the Cardinals and 49ers in Mexico City. Two years later games were held in London; in 2023 Frankfurt joined the list of venues. For the 2024 season, Goodell announced, "Brazil has established itself as a key market for the NFL, and we are excited to be playing in Brazil and São Paulo for the first time in 2024. Bringing the NFL to new continents, countries and cities around the world is a critical element of our plan to continue to grow the game globally." The Packers face the Eagles in the first Brazil game, with a total of five games in three foreign countries during '24. In 2025, the NFL will stage a game in Spain, and Australia is among countries being evaluated for future sites.

The NFL has also crafted a marketing plan that draws fans year-round, not just during the actual season. The 2024 player draft, for example, conducted in Detroit during the otherwise dull month of April, drew more than 775,000 fans — more than 30 percent of whom traveled over 100 miles to attend. According to one study, they contributed $214 million to businesses in Detroit and the surrounding area. Meanwhile, 54 million people watched on television during the three-day event. And fantasy football was a key to the excitement, with best ball drafts launched to coincide with the actual NFL draft.

Millions of fantasy football players rely upon giant companies for online platforms on which the games are played. ESPN has the most seasonal players (over 12 million), while Yahoo also has a major presence (over 6 million). DraftKings and FanDuel have sponsorship arrangements with 28 of the NFL's 32 teams. Underdog Fantasy has gained popularity for its best ball fantasy format, allowing users to draft teams and compete without the need for weekly roster management. CBS operates a comprehensive fantasy football platform that also offers news updates for NFL fans. Dozens of other operators, including Sleeper and My Fantasy League, have captured shares of the business, which is growing at about 8.5% annually. It's so potent that the NFL created its own platform, NFL Fantasy (with roughly 2.5 million users).

♦ ♦ ♦

For an enterprise that dwells on statistics, fantasy football doesn't have many good ones about itself. The stat cited earlier — that over 50 million Americans play some form of fantasy football — is, at best, a ballpark estimate. It is derived from data published by the Fantasy Sports & Gaming Association (FSGA) trade group, showing that as of 2023 there were 55.7 million Americans, aged 18 and older, participating in all fantasy sports. A survey showed that roughly 80 percent of them played fantasy football, producing a 44 million total. When ages 13 to 18 are included — as they were in earlier surveys — as many as eight million more players are added.

The global data company Statista looked into fantasy sports in 2022 and put the number of football participants at 29.2 million, considerably fewer than the FSGA's number but still, according to Statistica, making football "the most-played U.S. fantasy sport by a significant margin."

The FSGA study, conducted in early 2024 by the Angus Reid Group, showed a significant overlap between fantasy sports and formal sports wagering. Thirty-two percent of those surveyed said they had participated in fantasy or placed a bet in the previous 12 months. Nearly half (42 percent) are crossover players who have engaged in both.

Beyond hard data there is compelling anecdotal evidence about the scope of fantasy sports. For instance, the Fantasy Sports Writers Association, founded in 2004, now has over 1,100 members and in 2023 received more than 1,000 nominations for its annual awards. (The football writer of the year in '23 was Adam Harstad, whose thoughtful pieces appear on the Footballguys site. He's self-described as one who, "Eschews obfuscation. Espouses elucidation. Writes about football. Kisses and tells.")

In 2019, Bob Lung, who has written about fantasy football since 2002, organized The Fantasy Football Expo, in the city where he was born and raised — but best known for a sports landmark: the Pro Football Hall of Fame in Canton, Ohio. Lung had high hopes for the event, since it was planned for August to coincide with the annual induction ceremonies at the Hall. To his dismay, only 75 people showed up.

The following year Covid wiped out everything. "I really thought it was dead," Lung told me. "I really didn't think this would ever get off the ground." But then the Expo caught on and for the three-day event in 2024 more than 1,000 people were expected to attend. "We have 50 trade show booths," says Lung. "We have panel discussions all day long on Sunday about fantasy football and it's just kind of a family reunion for fans." Lung candidly notes that he makes a profit on the event, yet he's determined to keep it affordable for average fans.

According to Matthew Berry, arguably the master among fantasy football experts:

Bob Lung rallies visitors at the Fantasy Expo in Canton.

"The best part of fantasy is that it gives people who normally would not have reason to interact an excuse to talk. From the CEO and mailroom guys to long-lost cousins to everyone in between, they all have one thing in common: Fantasy brings them together. And it keeps them together too."

CHAPTER 2
Fun and Games

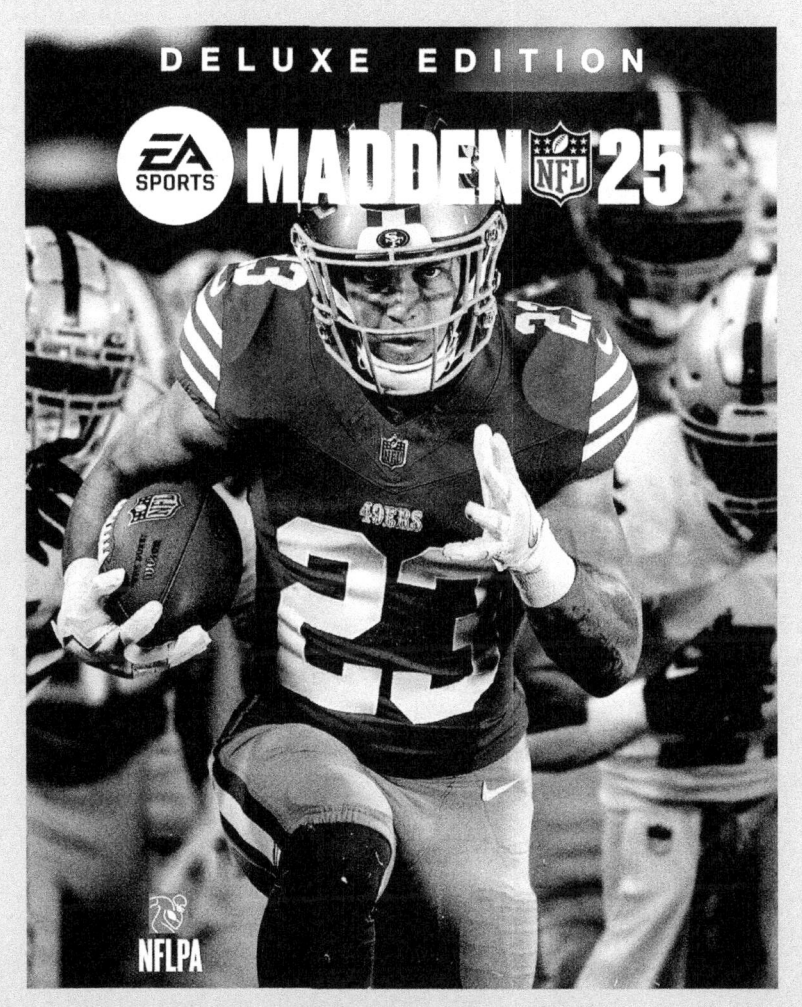

CMC runs for cover on Madden 25.

Origin stories of fantasy sports are fuzzy and sometimes contradictory.

In the broadest sense, you could say fantasy games include anything that allows participants to simulate a sport while not actually playing it. Dipping back to the 1800s, these can be summarized in four categories:

Parlor games: Reliant purely on chance, using dice, coins or cards, the earliest of which were related to baseball and date back to the 1860s, with football versions emerging circa 1890.

Probability games: Using the names of real players and their career stats to affect the odds, but with outcomes still dependent on chance — for example, with the spin of a wheel — and developed in the 1930s.

Results-based games: Combining names of real players with their actual stats in seasonal, weekly or daily play, evolving into fantasy-style football games in the 1960s.

Computer-assisted games: Adding technology to one or more of the above formats to enhance existing games or create new ones — launched on a mass scale in the mid-1980s with the development of the internet.

The first known sports parlor game — at least the first to be sold commercially — was invented in the mid-1860s by a baseball player named Francis C. Sebring, who pitched for the

Empire Base Ball Club of New York. As the story has it, Sebring was visiting an ailing teammate when he stumbled on the notion of a table-top game that would simulate action on the real diamond. Made of wood, the game involved "pitching" a coin with a spring-loaded paddle (similar to a pinball machine) and "batting" it with another paddle to propel it into the "field" where it might fall into one of several circular holes, signifying a "hit." Sebring called his game Parlor Base-Ball, according to a patent application filed in February 1868. Research shared with me by John Thorn, Major League Baseball's official historian, includes an ad placed by Masonic Manufacturing Co., describing Sebring's game:

> "Everything connected with it is so entirely original and so very different from most games, that it has the unqualified approbation of all who have used them. Pitching, batting, catching, and all the principal points of the great national game are played on these Field Boards."

About six months earlier a New Yorker named William Buckley had received a patent covering a similar game called Base-Ball Table, using marbles rather than coins. He described it as "... a new game for parlor or other indoor amusement ... played according to the rules and regulations of base-ball." Not much is known about Buckley, but it appears that he created his game after Sebring, yet beat him to the patent office. Regardless, Buckley's version never went into production while Sebring's did.

Rick Burton, who teaches "Baseball in American Culture" at Syracuse University believes these crude games planted seeds

INSIDE FANTASY FOOTBALL /37

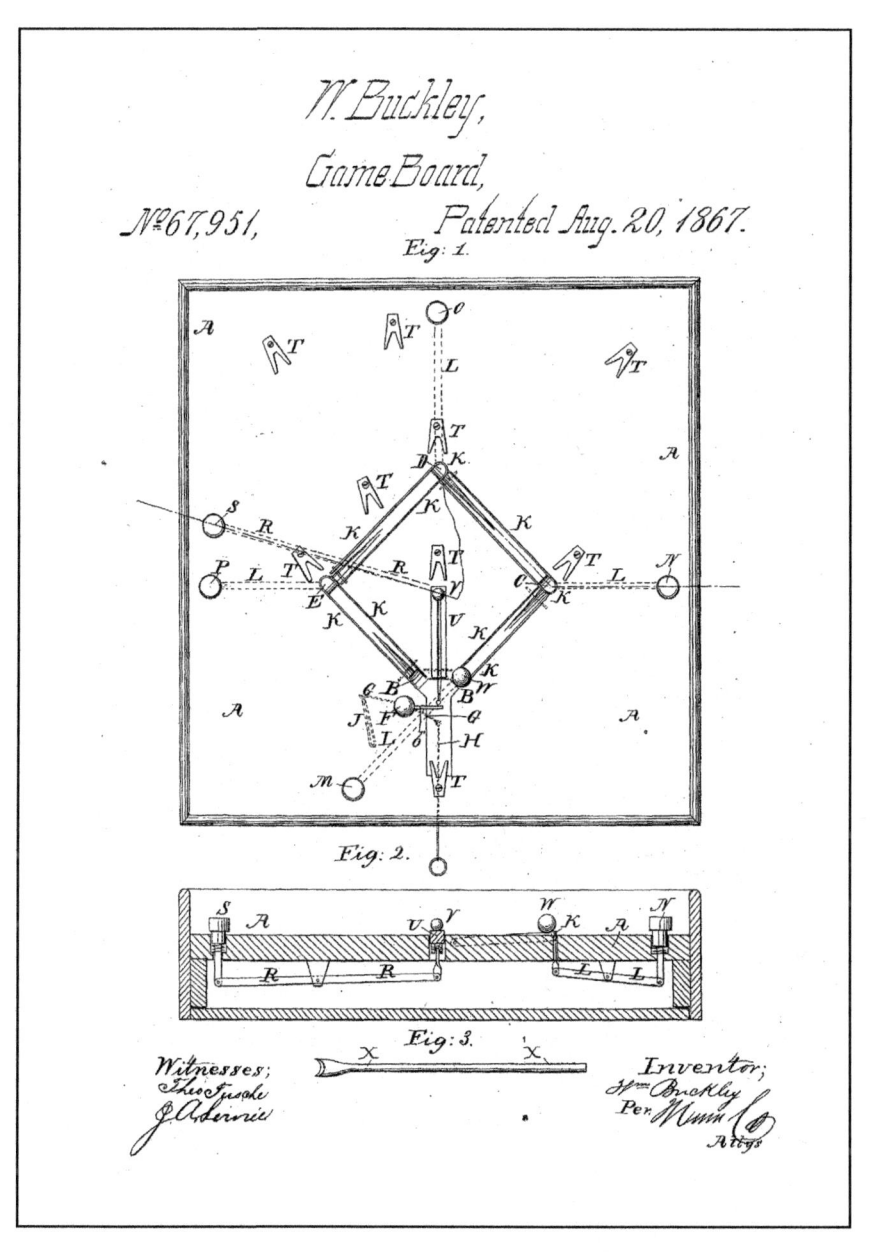

The patent drawing submitted by William Buckley for his Base-Ball Table.

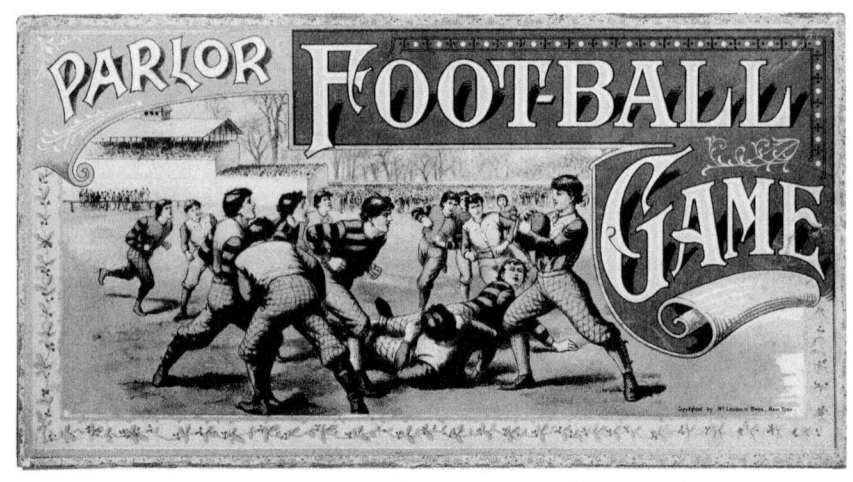

The tabletop game from McLoughlin Brothers.

that grew into today's fantasy sports. "If I play with a friend," he told me, "I can say, well, these are the players I want. I'm not saying that's what happened, but I'm saying it's feasible. They might have said, I'm going to be the Cincinnati Red Stockings or the New York Knickerbockers. If nothing else, they could take the starting lineups and assemble the batting order the way they wanted to as if they were the manager."

Tabletop football games came along about two decades after tabletop baseball, beginning with the attractively designed Parlor Foot-ball Game, created in 1891 by McLoughlin Brothers. Based in New York City, the firm specialized in children's books and games, notable for their advanced color printing. Laura Wasowicz, a curator with the American Antiquarian Society, located a copy of Parlor Foot-ball in the Hartford Civic Center's basement. "Its magnificently chromolithographed cover is nothing short of arresting," she writes. "It is the team jerseys that reveal more about the players and place of football in American

Tom Hamilton's game from Parker Brothers.

culture during the Gilded Age. Half of them wear the 'Y' of the Yale University Bulldogs, while the other half sport the orange and black horizontally striped jerseys of the Princeton University Tigers."

According to McLoughlin's instructions, "A piece, called a ball, and eleven men for each side, are used. The rules follow those of the regular game of collegiate football as closely as possible, deviating from them only insofar as simplicity absolutely requires." Players took turns spinning in order to advance the ball piece toward the opponent's goal line and maneuver around the blocking of four player pieces per team. In 1920 McLoughlin Brothers was acquired by Milton Bradley & Company, which discontinued the line of sports games and struggled with its own products as the Great Depression took hold.

The next major development in football gaming occurred in 1935 when Parker Brothers released a game called Tom Hamilton's Pigskin, named after a player-turned-coach at the U.S.

Naval Academy. (The game was somewhat under-publicized, considering that it came out the same year Parker Brothers released a product related to high finance, with the catchy title Monopoly.) Having a real-life celebrity endorse Pigskin marked a new phase in sports gaming — and was another precursor of fantasy football.

Three years later the legendary college coach Pop Warner lent his name to the Regulation Football Game. The makers boasted it was "Endorsed and played by leading football coaches." Using 100 cards with 800 "actual plays," the product was described as "the only game ever invented and patented as played with cards in the home that uses regular football rules and gives the same thrill when played scientifically as is experienced by the football fan when attending a regular football game."

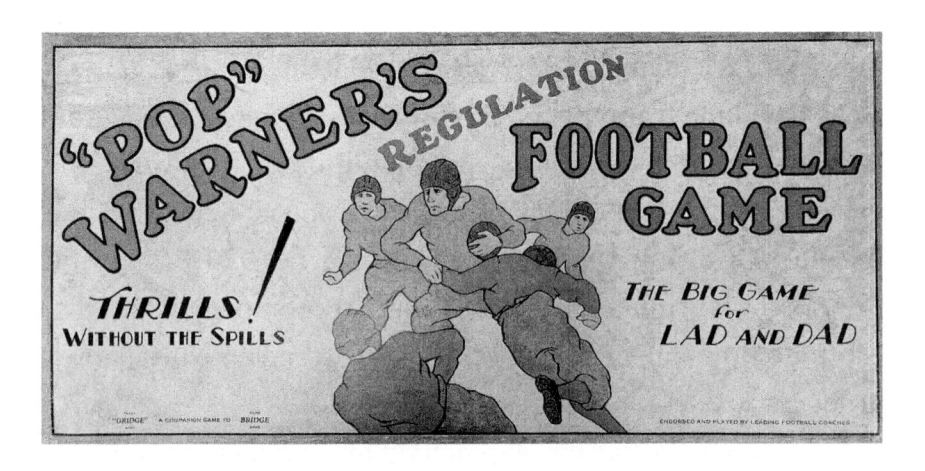

♦ ♦ ♦

Pop Warner lent his name to "Regulation Football."

Steve Anderson, a Minnesota businessman, played football board games as a kid and in 2000 began collecting them as a serious hobby. When his collection reached 250 games he chronicled them in a picture book, "Steve Anderson's Retro Football Games."

I asked him about the early links to fantasy football. "The games ultimately were about getting an outcome," he explains. "You pick 'A,' your opponent picks 'B,' then you look for an outcome. There were a couple of games in the sixties, one called APBA, and one called Strat-O-Matic, where, even to this day, there are some groups you can see on Facebook that play the games. They created their own leagues. So from that standpoint, I guess it'd be a precursor just because people were interested in football, they're playing a game and they're accumulating points, and there's a winner. From a competitive standpoint, from an interest in football standpoint, yes. But obviously, much less sophisticated."

Anderson cites the 1927 product, Woolsey's Foot Ball Game, in which a mechanical figurine, looking like a placekicker, is used. A ball is placed at his feet, and the figure tries to "kick" the ball into one of the holes of the bi-fold board. One of the more unusual items in his collection is Rotolette Foot-Ball, a 1933 game that uses a metal spinner and dials to determine the play and yardage. The 1946 Los Angeles Rams Football Game touted itself as a "Game of Skill! Not a Game of Chance!" a not so subtle tweak of its competitors. Rummy Football in 1946 utilized a standard deck of playing cards.

When the annual American Toy Fair was held in March of 1949, the buzz — quite literally — was electric football, a type of game that moved players on a gridiron board by vibration. The initial entry was Tru-Action, produced by Tudor Metal Products, followed into the market a few years later by games manufactured by Gotham Pressed Steel Corporation and sold through the popular Sears and Montgomery Ward catalogs. By 1959, Tudor was selling $1 million worth of electric games annually. The following year it received a licensing offer from NFL Enterprises, but turned it down and the deal subsequently went to Gotham. The resulting game, Gotham Official National League Electric Football G-1500, featured a four-inch high bright white metal frame that contained the NFL shield, plus the names of all NFL teams. The metal grandstand was patterned after Yankee Stadium where the football Giants played. It was as close to a complete fantasy experience as a fan in that era could hope for.

By the 1960s the NFL endorsed several board games, such as this product from the Ideal Toy Corporation.

Steve Anderson says the electric games helped make the stretch from 1950 to 1975 a Golden Age of football tabletop games, a period when more complex board games like APBA Football and Strat-O-Matic also came along. The field expanded rapidly to include such entries as Donald Duck Tricky Toe game in 1965 that had the Disney character kicking field goals. An Official Football Chess game in 1967 used chess pieces as football players. Also in '67, De Luxe Topper Corporation introduced a robot in its game, Charley 'n Me. Charley is "the world's greatest computerized pre-programmed robot," who can play games with kids "just like a human being." In 1969, Marx produced Pro Bowl Live Action Football using a 7-foot plastic playing field mat, with 4-inch plastic figures.

The 1970s saw the development of games that used audio components. One of Anderson's favorites was a Mattel product, appropriately named Talking Football, that came with play-by-play recordings of calls by none other than legendary broadcaster Dick Enberg.

"You started getting the battery operated handheld games with the basic chips, and the computer age came into being in the '80s," says Anderson, "so sports board games kind of became passé. I think today's fantasy football is much more social. You know, I've got this group of 12 buddies, and we're into it, and we're giving each other a hard time."

There were dozens of popular video games like NES Play Action Football, Tom Landry Strategy Football, NFL Quarterback Club 98 and NFL 2K. But the undisputed king — and the one that still flourishes today — is the one that bears the name of the late coach and broadcaster John Madden.

The game was the creation of Trip Hawkins, who founded Electronic Arts in 1982. On a train ride from Denver to Oakland, Hawkins chatted with Madden about a football simulation video game that would be a 7-on-7 contest. "If it was going to be me and going to be pro football, it had to have 22 guys on the screen," Madden later told ESPN. "If we couldn't have that, we couldn't have a game." Hawkins developed a more realistic game, which was called John Madden Football and debuted in 1988 for the Apple II computer. Today, the Madden NFL series of video games continues to sell millions of copies annually, has generated more than $7 billion in revenue and helped turn EA into one of the world's most prominent gaming companies. The company selected fantasy football's hottest star, 49ers running back Christian McCaffrey, for the cover of "Madden NFL 25," making him the first RB in a decade to receive the honor. CMC tweeted, "Lifelong Dream Come True!"

I met Madden, who died in 2021, on several occasions and took note — as we all did — of his infectious enthusiasm for the game, both on the field and on the screen. He commented as energetically when he and I sat and watched a high school baseball game in Monterey, California, as he did at a Super Bowl. With his video games, Madden demanded realism, instructing developers on details as exacting as how a defensive player should be tackling and which stances linemen should use during certain formations.

Madden was a fan of fantasy football, having befriended Bill Winkenbach, its inventor, as we'll see in the next chapter. Today Madden's video products have bridged the gap, with DraftKings offering simulated contests with cash prizes and, since

2022, live streams of simulated games on Twitch.

Summing up his remarkable career, John Madden put it this way: "If someone remembers me as a coach, they still call me 'Coach,' but if they know me for the video game, they just call me 'Madden.'"

After Madden's death on December 28, 2021, Electronic Arts put him on the cover of the game for the first time in over 20 years.

CHAPTER 3

They Called it 'GOPPPL'

Bill Winkenbach, the man who invented fantasy football.

The 1962 Oakland Raiders football team was so bad that for management and media the idea of winning was pure fantasy.

Born out of desperation in 1960, a few months before the inaugural season of the eight-team American Football League, the franchise was formed after Minnesota's AFL entry jumped to the well-established National Football League. A "Name Your Football Team" contest, conducted by the *Oakland Tribune*, produced as finalists: Admirals, Lakers, Diablos, Seawolves, Gauchos, Nuggets, Señors, Dons, Costers, Grandees, Sequoias, Missiles, Knights, Redwoods, Clippers, Jets and Dolphins. A selection committee announced that the winning choice was "Señors," immediately prompting ridicule because the team's managing partner, Chet Soda, had an annoying habit of calling guys "señor." Nine days later the name was changed to "Raiders."

The University of California refused to allow the upstarts to play home games at Memorial Stadium in Berkeley, forcing the Raiders to scramble for accommodations across the bay in San Francisco, with some games at Kezar Stadium and others at Candlestick Park. Attendance was low, the team lost money, and several of the original owners bailed out.

Though the Raiders managed to win six of 14 games in 1960, the following year they slumped to 2-12 — and season three was even worse. After five games coach Marty Feldman was fired, just as the team departed for a three-city East Coast swing. By the time the Raiders landed in a storm at New York's Idlewild Airport in November 1962 for a game against the Titans (later named the Jets), the mood was as lousy as the Raiders' 0-7 record and spirits as damp as the weather.

After hustling through the TWA terminal, members of the traveling party ran up a hefty bar tab at a Manhattan hotel later known as the Milford Plaza and more recently Row NYC. Present were Scotty Stirling, beat writer for the *Oakland Tribune*, Bill Tunnell of the Raiders front office staff and, for a portion of the evening, George Ross, the *Tribune* sports editor. Leading the discussion was Wilfred "Bill" Winkenbach, a prominent Bay Area businessman and a minority owner of the Raiders. In the 1950s Winkenbach had developed a game involving PGA Tour golf in which fans like himself would "draft" pro players and then add up their weekly scores to determine a winner. A few years later he came up with a version for baseball, utilizing stats for pitching and home runs. On this gloomy night in New York, the focus was football and how to construct a game that would allow participants to roster stars from both pro leagues (the established NFL and the new AFL) — players like Jim Brown, Mike Ditka and Frank Gifford.

By morning they had invented fantasy football.

Returning home they formed the Greater Oakland Professional Pigskin Prognosticators League — the GOPPPL.

"Though I was involved, Winkenbach deserves the lion's share of the credit for developing the game," Stirling said later. "We chipped in with rules, but the germ of inspiration was these earlier games he played with golf and baseball."

There is no record of the group using the term "fantasy," which would enter the sports lexicon years later. But the concepts drawn up that night are the essence of the game played today around the world, a game embraced by the NFL and its players, media, and tens of millions of fans, with scope and intensity that Winkenbach and his chums never imagined.

♦ ♦ ♦

Born in East Oakland in 1911, Bill Winkenbach played some sandlot baseball and like many youngsters fantasized about being a Major Leaguer. He took a few courses at UC Berkeley and wound up working in shipyards as an estimator of ceramic tiles. His business savvy proved far better than his baseball swing and before long he was an owner of Superior Tile Company. In the early sixties his love of sports coupled with civic pride led Winkenbach to invest in the Raiders, despite fearing that the team — and perhaps the entire AFL — wouldn't survive for long competing with the powerful NFL.

The Raiders were a depressing mess, finishing the '62 season 1-13, but that didn't diminish enthusiasm for GOPPPL, which held its first draft the following summer. The fantasy league was composed of Raiders staff, local sports writers and a few season ticket holders, 16 people in all — eight managers and eight assistants — two of whom ended up as actual NFL general managers: Ron Wolf with the Packers and Scotty Stirling with the Raiders. Stirling was a two-sport GM, working in that capacity for the Golden State Warriors and New York Knicks. The original list of GOPPPL owners also included radio announcer Bob Blum and ticket manager George Glace, along with his assistants Phil Carmona and Ralph Casebolt.

They played for pennies (a touchdown was worth 50 cents) but their larger purpose was promotion. GOPPPL's original charter stated, "It is felt that this tournament will automatically increase closer coverage of daily happenings in professional football." That one sentence became fundamental in the evolution of fantasy football. It was started by people who loved football and sought to promote the game on the field, but for many years it was scorned by the NFL itself and ignored by media, due in part to its links to gambling. Decades later, as we'll see, the sports world bought in — literally — and embraced fantasy football with the very promotional goals that Winkenbach's group envisioned.

"Prior to the opening of the professional football season," the GOPPPL rules stated, "club owners will draft 20 players from either league. However, no more than eight imports can be drafted from the NFL." Remember, everyone in GOPPPL was connected to the Raiders in the newly formed AFL, thus the snide term "imports."

As for drafting, the rules stipulated:

"At the first draft, cards will be cut for first choice, second choice, etc. The last choice or eighth choice will also get ninth choice going back up the ladder. Thus, the first choice will get sixteenth and seventeenth choice. After all cuts have been made, each owner will declare in what position he wants to draft. The following year, first choice goes to the heaviest loser of the preceding year and so forth." This system, now referred to as a "snake draft," was one of many innovations from the sixties league that remains in use on many fantasy platforms today.

Each GOPPPL owner selected a total of four offensive ends, four halfbacks, two fullbacks, two quarterbacks, two kickoff or punt return men, two field goal kickers, two defensive backs or linebackers and two defensive linemen. From this roster, owners submitted a weekly starting lineup featuring two offensive ends, two halfbacks, a fullback and a quarterback. "Bill would sit together with the other limited partners at home Raider games," Stirling recalled, "and for the first couple of weeks of the season their big concern was not how the Raiders were doing, but how well their GOPPPL team was playing."

The first GOPPPL draft sheet, compiled in Bill Winkenbach's basement in August, 1963. Houston's George Blanda, who played both quarterback and kicker, went first.

Gerald Winkenbach remembers his father setting up radios around the family television, so he could watch one away game and listen to others. "He was a diehard fan," adds daughter, Patty. "Loved all sports but totally got into football. Sunday was football day as much as church day."

Using a wood lathe in his shop, Winkenbach made a trophy with a wooden football face and a dunce cap on top for the team that came in last each year. "The last-place guy had to keep it on his mantle till the next season," said Stirling, "and when you visited his house he damn well better have that trophy up on the mantle or there was trouble."

Though limited to paper and pencil in the pre-computer era, Winkenbach prepared detailed weekly stat reports that were delivered to GOPPPL owners on Tuesday mornings. "He'd start Sunday night phoning the *San Francisco Examiner* sports desk," Gerald told me. "And when they got tired of giving him statistics he'd call the *Chronicle*. Then he'd go to the *Oakland Tribune*. There was no internet, so it took him hours to do this.

"Dad became friends with John Madden," said Gerald, referring to the legendary coach and then broadcaster, who worked at San Diego State before joining the Raiders staff in '66. "Eventually, dad talked John and his wife Virginia into buying a condo at the golf course in Boulder Creek. Saturday mornings they'd meet at the clubhouse restaurant and talk football. I imagine my father was picking up advice about who to take in the GOPPPL draft."

The annual draft was moved from Winkenbach's basement to a popular Oakland restaurant — where the menu improved dramatically. According to invitations sent out by

When the Raiders won their first Super Bowl in 1977, John Madden held the trophy with friend and GOPPPL founder, Bill Winkenbach, on hand (far right).

Winkenbach in 1966, participants had their choice of Prime Rib or New York steak at $6 per person, tax and gratuity included. Attendees at the 1967 draft dinner could choose between sirloin steak, prime rib or lobster thermidor for $11 per couple.

One of the original GOPPPL coaches, recruited by Stirling, was an Oakland bar owner named Andy Mousalimas. "We were pro football addicts when nobody in the East Bay knew about pro football," Mousalimas recalled years later. "So one day, Scotty comes in and says, 'I have a good game for you. I want you to join this GOPPPL.' I said, 'fine.' But I didn't know what the heck he was talking about."

With the No. 1 overall pick in '63, Stirling and Mousalimas took Houston quarterback/kicker George Blanda, who had thrown 36 touchdown passes two years earlier. In doing so, the duo passed on Jim Brown, who went to Ross at No. 2. GOPPPL rules awarded 50 cents for rushing touchdowns, 25 cents for touchdown receptions, and double those amounts for any scoring play longer than 75 yards. Brown rushed for 12 touchdowns in 1963, including an 80-yard scoring run. He averaged 6.4 yards per carry and totalled 1,863 rushing yards, breaking his own single-season record. As a result Ross won the first GOPPPL title, while Stirling and Mousalimas finished in last place.

◆ ◆ ◆

Andrew Mousalimas was a hero in World War II, so accomplished that Adolf Hitler personally put a price on his head. As a member of an elite commando unit of the Office of Strategic Services, Mousalimas and his comrades secretly parachuted behind enemy lines into occupied Greece and disrupted German forces, destroying infrastructure and pinning down more than two dozen German divisions that otherwise would have been sent to France to stop the Allied invasion on D-Day. In response, Hitler issued his infamous Fuhrer Order No. 003830: "From now on, all enemies on so-called commando missions are to be slaughtered to the last man. Even if these individuals should apparently be prepared to give themselves up, no pardon is to be granted them." For his heroics Mousalimas was awarded the Congressional Gold Medal.

After the war he came back home to Oakland and managed a bar on Telegraph Avenue named the Lamp Post, one of the few such establishments in the area that would serve minorities. He sold it in 1968 and, along with his wife and brother-in-law, purchased a bar called the King's X on Piedmont Avenue, giving

The King's X bar in Oakland.

it the vibe of an English pub. A gregarious presence, Mousalimas created a big Greek family for the regulars. Columnist Chip Johnson once wrote in the *San Francisco Chronicle*, "The King's X is a bar, complete with all the trappings you'd expect to find in a quality establishment. They have gin rummy tournaments, liar's dice, sports contests, a jamming jukebox, wise-guy bartenders and heavy drinkers, including a few who probably border on the clinical definition of alcoholics. What else could you possibly want from a bar?"

Mousalimas took his knowledge of the GOPPPL game and set up fantasy football leagues at his establishment, explaining in a 2012 interview with ESPN, "In all humility, I think the King's X is what really perpetuated it in the Bay Area. No question, Wink was the godfather. The only trouble with Wink was that he didn't want to make any changes to the rules. He was stubborn as hell. Damn, he was stubborn. In the GOPPPL, a return touchdown was 250 points and a receiving touchdown was 25 points. So I formed a rules committee to update the game. We were the first ones to put in a yardage rule. You had guys like Pete Banaszak, who would carry the ball four or five times and score two to three touchdowns from the 1-yard line, while you had other guys like O.J., who was running wild, but he wasn't scoring, so he wasn't getting any points. We fixed that."

On Sunday nights Mousalimas would close the bar at 2 a.m. and wait until 4 when the *Tribune* and *Chronicle* were delivered to DeLauer's newsstand so he could pore over box-scores and post the stats. As the task grew, with as many as 200 leagues among his patrons, he'd save an hour by going directly to the Tribune plant at 3 a.m. to grab a paper as it came off the press.

His one ironclad rule was that players had to show up in person at the bar on Friday night before 10 p.m. to set their rosters for the weekend. "I used to love Friday nights," Mousalimas said. "There might be three guys owning one team, but they'd all come in on Friday nights. Everybody showed up, and the place rocked. On Sundays we had a sign: '$13.75 — breakfast, bus and a ticket to the Raiders.' I'd have as many as four buses going to the Raiders games.

"There was no talk radio, there was no internet," he recalled. "It was tough to do research, and we worked hard to find information." He'd phone newspapers in other cities hoping to get tips from beat reporters but was often rebuffed as the journalists, unfamiliar with fantasy sports, assumed he was a bookie.

The King's X became a Bay Area hotbed of fantasy foot-

Andy Mousalimas in a 2012 photo, wearing his jacket from the Toyota Hall of Fame: Legends of Fantasy Football.

ball, featuring six divisions: The Kings Division (est. 1969); the X Division (est. 1970); the Taxi Division (est. 1971); the Other Division (est. 1971); the Rookie Division (est. 1973); and the Queens Division (est. 1973), a division started exclusively for women. "Listen, I love the ladies," Mousalimas insisted, "but I would not let them participate in the draft. I felt that this was a man's night out. But the ladies got all upset. A good friend of mine, Albert Santini, said, 'You know, Andy, why don't you start an all-ladies division?' I think his wife had talked to him. I said, 'That sounds like a good idea,' and you know what? The ladies turned out to be the most loyal of the whole group."

♦ ♦ ♦

GOPPPL continues to this day with Stan Heeb, who joined in 1974, as its commissioner. "Fantasy gives us lay people a vehicle to show our expertise in putting a team together," he told me. "It's also about competitiveness. Many people in fantasy football are either ex-athletes, or wannabe athletes. Now they can compete, they can show their knowledge of sports. It's a huge part of my life. I love sports. It's a way to stay involved. With fantasy, I watch football games a lot differently than I used to."

I asked Heeb about the term "fantasy football," which he says was never used back at the start. "We just called the game 'The Draft,'" he said. GOPPPL, which currently consists of 10 teams, retains most of the basic scoring system invented by Winkenbach.

"Basically 50 cents for a touchdown," Heeb explained. "If it's a passing touchdown, the quarterback gets 25 and the receiver gets 25. If it's a rushing touchdown, whoever rushes it in, no matter what position they are, they get the whole 50 cents. Now, if the touchdown is over 75 yards you get double, so if they run the touchdown in 80 yards, you get a buck rather than 50 cents. If the quarterback throws it, the quarterback gets 50 and the receiver gets 50. Field goals are 25, double if it's over 50 yards. Extra points are worth 10, and you get 20 for a two-point conversion. Defense and special teams touchdowns are worth a dollar; safeties 20 cents."

Are we talking about actual money or just monopoly?

"Actual money. If a guy scores, say, 350 in a week, then the other people just subtract — my team scores 250, and your team scores 350, I owe you a buck. And we keep track of all that week to week. At the end, the leader is usually anywhere from 70 to 100 bucks ahead, but there are side bets, based on your position. Everyone pays the winner 30 bucks, and 20 bucks to every other team ahead of you. So if you come in last, you're owing nine teams. The winner takes home around 250 to 350 bucks. So it's not a money thing, you know, money isn't really a big factor."

Heeb and his compatriots still harbor resentment over the place given in fantasy history to Rotisserie baseball — a creation of journalist Daniel Okrent in 1979. For many years, mainstream outlets such as ESPN cited it as the first evidence of fantasy sports which, of course, it was not. The GOPPPL started in 1963, and before that Winkenbach played a crude form of fantasy baseball. Also, in 1960 a Harvard sociology professor William Gamson developed "Baseball Seminar," a game in which he and his colleagues would pick players and assign points to their batting average, RBIs, wins and ERA. Gamson later exported the game to the University of Michigan, where history professor Bob Sklar became an avid player of the Baseball Seminar, which also became known on campus as the "Assistant Professor League" or the "Untenured Faculty League." During the 1968 school year one of Sklar's students in American Studies was Daniel Okrent, who learned about the game.

When Okrent eventually started his own league it contained some of Gamson's rules and used the adopted name "Rotisserie" because the managers met at La Rotisserie Francaise restaurant in New York City. However, Okrent later clarified that the primary conversation about the game actually took place at another Manhattan restaurant, P.J. Moriarity's. Regarding the lasting tale about La Rotisserie, Okrent said, "The place meant nothing to us. We never went back there. It had no continuing meaning at all. We should have called the game Moriarity Baseball, and let the publicity from our league keep that lousy restaurant in business instead of the other lousy one."

◆ ◆ ◆

The true founders of fantasy football remained passionate about the game throughout their lives.

Bill Winkenbach never profited from his creation, the offshoots of which are now worth billions. Shortly before his death in 1993 at 81, Winkenbach ran into Scotty Stirling and quipped, "I told you we should have copyrighted the damn thing." Indeed, his children, Gerald and Patty, told me they sought legal advice about making some sort of claim to the fantasy football concept. "We learned from an attorney," Gerald explained, "that the problem with a game is that someone can change just one rule and then your copyright isn't any good. Besides, my dad was only in it for fun. He wasn't crazy about the growing financial elements in all aspects of sports."

Andy Mousalimas, who died in 2020 at 95, was asked if he had any regrets.

"Only one," he said. "I should have drafted Jim Brown."

CHAPTER 4

A Whole New Ballgame

"THE TALENTED MR. ROTO"

Let the trash talking begin

And so the butler was taken away, never having realized the person he had killed ... was his long-lost brother!

That's for those of you who have just skipped to the end of the magazine. Hah! I just ruined the ending. Serves you right.

For the rest of you ... whew. How was it? Good for you? You've come to the end of the inaugural RotoWorld.com Fantasy Football Draft Guide. How do you feel? Hopefully, you are psyched for a great draft and a winning season. Those losers in your league who tell you they play for fun are full of it. If they were just playing for fun, they wouldn't want to keep score and make fun of you when you start a bye-week player. No, it is more fun when you win - and you'll win more frequently with RotoWorld.com's powerful information behind you. Let the trash talking begin!

Don't stop studying now, though! I would love to tell you that we can see the future, that nothing has changed at all since this magazine went to press, but that, of course, wouldn't be likely. I mean, Fred Taylor was still healthy as I wrote this. What are the odds of that staying true?

But it's all good. You have Fantasy Football Draft insurance in your hands. You bought a magazine from a 24/7 website skilled in updating news, depth charts and cheat sheets on every action in the NFL pre-season. If an RB gets hurt, he is off the cheat sheets, out of the depth charts, on the online-specific content as well. Also, we will be running an expert's advice section online along with other interesting features that allow you to interact with your peers. Secondly, you can personalize reports. We give you five years of data to sort any way you please. Each report will allow you to go back up to five years and sometimes include both projections and 2002 stats on the same page. We also have updated news, transactions, injury reports and deeper team oriented features that could not be included in the magazine.

Knowledge is power. Anyone can have knowledge through memorization of the facts in this publication and on our website. It is analysis that changes "knowledge" to "application" or "having power" to "being powerful." So, yeah ... BE POWERFUL. Apply the knowledge, skill and cunning to be the champion of your fantasy football league! That's the kind of people we are, at RotoWorld.com. We want to help you win, by turning simple facts and knowledge into POWER!

Well, I really want to thank you for your continued support of RotoWorld.com. We recognize that without you, we would not be able to take this leap into print publishing. We hope that you like our approach, analysis, projections and statistics. Most of all, we hope this was entertaining and that we will help you have more fun in your fantasy football league. If there's any way that we can

> **Most of all, we hope this was entertaining and that we will help you have more fun in your fantasy football league.**

The inaugural issue of RotoWorld's annual fantasy draft guide, published in July of 2003.

Without much media coverage to stimulate interest, fantasy football made a slow crawl across the country during a two-decade period following GOPPPL's creation in 1963. It caught on mostly where guys gathered: on college campuses and at places of business — but even for rabid NFL fans, drafting and setting weekly lineups was enormously time-consuming and frustratingly imprecise. All too often there were cases of fantasy managers selecting a player in August only to learn later that he had retired at the end of the previous season. Fantasy lore even includes a few cases of draft picks who turned out to be deceased.

Relief came in the mid-1980s as several fantasy buffs in different corners of the country almost simultaneously hit on the idea of publishing annual guides — and soon after that weekly magazines — to educate fantasy managers.

Among the pioneers were buddies who met at St. Paul Johnson Senior High in Minnesota: Tom Kane Jr. and Cliff Charpentier. Working out of Charpentier's mother's basement in 1983 they created and self-published a book called *Fantasy Football Digest*. The first issue, focusing on the 1984 NFL season, was distributed only in Minnesota yet sold a remarkable 3,000 copies.

"In the early days of fantasy football — the '80s, way before the internet, when there were maybe one-fiftieth of the number of players there are now — there was almost nothing published about fantasy football," says Paul Charchian, another Minnesotan, who a decade later launched *Fantasy Football Weekly* magazine and went on to become president of the Fantasy Sports & Gaming Association, while developing other fantasy sports products.

"There was nothing on TV, there was nothing on radio," he recalls. "If you wanted any kind of advice on fantasy football, the only place to go to was Cliff Charpentier's *Digest*. For those of us who were playing back then, it's hard to overstate just how important that one book was. Those guys deserve a lot of credit for helping popularize fantasy sports."

Kane ran the business side, while Charpentier did the writing. The first issue, an impressive paperback-style book priced at $7.95, promised: "A look at the game ... How to start your own league ... Variations of the game ... A guide for the fantasy football draft '84 ... Drafting strategies ... Rating the players ... Complete player stats ... 1984 NFL schedule." The *Digest* also provided insights from Charpentier himself. In the '84 edition, for example, this was the entry for Houston Oilers quarterback Warren Moon:

> *Moon (HOUS) — Hard to say how this Canadian Football League star will do in the NFL, but with Houston's additional acquisition of Butch Johnson from Dallas, look for a decent passing attack to compliment running of Earl Campbell.*

The first 18 issues of Fantasy Football Digest, beginning with the 1984 edition (upper left).

Aside from misspelling "complement," it was the kind of research that fantasy football managers craved — and back in the '80s found difficult to come by outside of their local markets. "I rated all the players, making it easy so the average NFL fan could play," Charpentier said. "We took away the work."

(For the record, Moon finished tenth in passing yards among NFL quarterbacks in '84. He became the first Black QB inducted into the Pro Football Hall of Fame.)

Charpentier and Kane soon struck a deal with a publishing company and *Fantasy Football Digest* went national, described by *USA Today* as "the Bible of fantasy football."

◆ ◆ ◆

At about the same time, two journalism students at the University of Washington, Ian Allan and Bruce Taylor, had similar ambitions. "We were in a class called Creativity and Innovation," Taylor told me. "You had to identify a service or a product that wasn't currently available. Ours was creating an annual preview magazine for people who play a sports statistics game called fantasy football." From their class project, for which they got a perfect 4.0 grade, emerged an actual magazine funded with $5,000 that had been left to Allan by his piano teacher. *Fantasy Football*, launched in 1987, achieved hefty national sales and the phones in its office were soon ringing continually as readers sought updates on player injuries or advice on setting lineups.

Allan and Taylor learned the magazine business out of necessity. Using the graduate school library at the University of Washington, they scoured local newspapers from around the county to compile NFL reports. They also studied the football yearbook published by Street and Smith and "borrowed" unabashedly from *Don Heinrich's Pro Preview*, which called itself, "The pro football annual for the serious fan!"

"We were in search of a formula," Taylor recalls, "and also trying to be irreverent. We had what you would expect: team by team breakdowns, and position by position breakdowns. Then we did things like our 'Stooge of the Year': players who were a cut above in last year's 'race for disgrace.' It was kind of over the top, and that was me. Ian wouldn't have written something that crappy, but I felt that piece put a finger on another thing that is an important motivation for fantasy coaches, which is the need to not be humiliated, the need to not screw up and subject yourself to ridicule from your buddies.

"We weren't just some MBA suits trying to fill a market need that had been identified through research and focus groups. We just wanted to make something that we wanted to have ourselves."

Surreptitiously using the school's WATS (Wide Area Telephone Service) line, they phoned 350 wholesalers seeking distribution for their $2.99 publication.

After a few years and a taste of success, Allan and Taylor became convinced that their magazine's name was too generic so they renamed it *Fantasy Football Index*, which continues to publish today.

◆ ◆ ◆

Dan and Kelly Grogan, brothers living in Colorado in 1985, joined a fantasy football league along with employees at a gas company. "We didn't do a whole lot of homework for our first draft," Kelly recalls. "We thought we knew something about football," adds Dan, "but there were no magazines about fantasy sports and the online world hadn't arrived yet." Their first draft pick was Miami quarterback Dan Marino — a safe choice, who a year earlier had been named the NFL's MVP. But in the fourth round the brothers stumbled badly, selecting Seattle wide receiver Paul Johns. They later learned Johns had suffered a neck injury the previous season and had been forced to retire. "We left the draft and sat in the car," says Dan, "and we said 'we just can't make mistakes like this anymore, so let's start compiling this information,'" The following year the brothers were surprised when a member of the league offered ten dollars for a copy of their handwritten notes.

That led to a typed version on legal-sized paper, with data about every NFL team. They left 10 copies at a local newsstand and within a few hours the dealer phoned to say all had been sold — at eight dollars per copy. The following year a more formal magazine took shape, with the title *Player Eval*. "We had no experience in publishing," notes Kelly — we still had other jobs — but we felt we were onto something." After changing the name to *Grogan's Fantasy Football* and hooking up with a national distributor, the press run climbed from 5,000 copies to 100,000, but even at that level the brothers encountered confusion about fantasy sports. "I remember calling one distributor," says Kelly, "and I told him about fantasy football, and he said, 'Sorry. We don't carry x-rated material.'"

◆ ◆ ◆

Jack Pullman worked as an accountant on the South Side of Chicago in the 1970s and was introduced to what his associates called "The Player Pool." They didn't know the term "fantasy football," which would come into use years later. He eventually formed his own league, taking note that, "there are all these football magazines on the market, but none of them are fantasy football magazines. I was thinking, 'What would I want to know to get ready for the season?'" He was reading Cliff Charpentier's newsletter but was unaware of Charpentier's more formal *Fantasy Football Digest*. In 1986 he launched All-Pro Publishing with the tagline, "If you play fantasy football to win you've got to be an all-pro!"

One of Pullman's clever maneuvers was using his own paying subscribers as stringers to gather information about their local NFL teams. "Back in the early days a lot of people knew a lot about their local teams from their local media. I gave these guys a 15 percent discount on a subscription and credit in print. They were terrific. It was one of the best things I ever did."

In 1982 the Gannett company launched the national daily newspaper *USA Today*, with a detailed sports section that for a time served as the stats bible for fantasy players. The paper also used its pages for fantasy games in which readers picked against a salary cap or selected players from particular talent groups. By late '85, *USA Today* had become the second-largest newspaper in the United States, reaching a daily circulation of 1.4 million copies. In 1990 *USA Today* joined forces with STATS Inc., which a few years earlier had converted itself into a data service delivering sports statistics to media and directly to fans.

◆ ◆ ◆

In 1993 Paul Charchian, who had majored in journalism in college, was doing tech work at an accounting firm in Minneapolis. He and a co-worker, both avid fantasy football players, took note of the fact that while there were several annual publications devoted to the game — like those covered above — and a few crude newsletters, there was no weekly, in-season fantasy football publication. With $10,000 seed money they launched *Fantasy Football Weekly*, a 24-page tabloid with a $2.50 cover price. It sold surprisingly well in Minnesota, as had been the case with Charpentier's *Fantasy Football Digest*, so in year two distribution was expanded to every NFL city. "Huge, huge mistake," says Charchian. "We found out that people in Florida or in California weren't playing. We lost so much money."

The debut issue of Fantasy Football Weekly in 1993.

What is it about Minnesota and fantasy football?

"A six month winter," he told me with a laugh. "There's not a lot else you can do. You become an avid indoorsman from October to April — and what better way to spend a good chunk of that than to play fantasy football? There were all these resources here that made it seem very popular. We had Cliff Charpentier's book when it was just selling regionally and locally. We had a radio show in the Twin Cities on Sunday night that would read box scores so commissioners could score their league on Sunday night instead of having to wait for the Monday morning paper. And we thought the whole nation was playing like we were playing here in the Twin Cities.

"Because it's a viral pastime, you know, the more leagues get created, and it grows and becomes a self-perpetuating cycle. There's some research out there suggesting that Minnesota still has the highest per capita participation rate for fantasy football in the nation."

♦ ♦ ♦

As important as the early print products were in popularizing fantasy football, it was the development of home computers and the internet that propelled the games in meteoric fashion. Among the pioneers were Patrick Hughes, a marketing exec at IBM and his brother, a computer programmer, who developed and marketed a software program to allow fantasy players to manage their teams electronically. Soon after the software appeared in stores in 1988, Hughes was approached by NFL Properties and told of a possible relationship with Miller Brewing Company, which led to "Miller Franchise Football."

Hughes would compile statistics every Monday, copies of which were delivered by FedEx to over 350 beer distributors for distribution to bars and taverns where the Miller game was offered. The following year, Miller hired legendary coach and commentator John Madden to pitch the product, and the number of participating bars soared to 6,500. "Essentially," Hughes says proudly, "that's what launched fantasy football nationwide." (In 2001 Hughes sold his business to Rupert Murdoch's News Corp.)

◆ ◆ ◆

Rick Wolf was working in 1987 as a programmer at Prodigy — a pre-internet dial-up venture that included CBS and IBM, along with retailer Sears, Roebuck and Company. He was part of the technology team that built production tools used to put ESPN on Prodigy in 1992 and helped develop the first online fantasy game, Baseball Manager. In 1995, Wolf was hired by SportsLine.com where he broke down the market into six types of fan: casual, team, fantasy, gambler, historian and collector. Their fantasy digital offering was marketed in three tiers. It contained a commissioner product so players could run a league with friends, a salary cap game that could be played online, and a content package which helped fantasy managers draft better and perform better in season. All three combined were sold for $99 and managed to attract about a half a million customers.

Grandstand Sports Services soon launched the first national fantasy football leagues online through Q-Link (later America Online). ESPN covered fantasy football in 1995 on SportsZone, ESPN's online site, but it didn't run leagues (something that didn't happen at ESPN until 2007). Beginning in 1997, fans could set up their leagues online via RotoNews (now Rotowire), Commissioner.com (later part of CBS Sports) and other sites that allowed them to follow stats in real time. SportSim, a free fantasy sports environment where players would pit their "dream team" against teams concocted by other players, was launched in '97 by CNN/SI, an internet venture born of a partnership between CNN and *Sports Illustrated*.

In 1997 *The Sporting News* acquired a product that allowed fans to customize their leagues in varying formats. In the past, fantasy managers had to play by the rules that the platform operator established. *The Sporting News* also integrated real-time statistical updates, allowing players to check back with the site during and after games for updates on their team. Several other companies entered the fantasy space, including Yahoo — which relied on its popular internet search engine and offered all of its games for free as part of a strategy to increase its internet penetration.

"When Yahoo came free," Wolf told me, "we made the decision to go free to break the market, so that they wouldn't be able to own it. Our strategy was enabled by, you guessed it, Miller Lite. They paid a sponsorship to make all fantasy leagues free on CBS Sportsline and we dragged in about three-and-a-half million people to use our Commissioner Services, with an estimated 59 percent of them playing for the first time. The following year, we turned it back to pay. We had them hooked into ours which was a lot better, and we just said, 'You get great value for this. So go play on the free one if you want. But now you've seen ours because we set it free. And now you're gonna want to keep it.' And basically, CBS Sportsline has been able to keep a large portion of those same customers for 20-plus years."

At a Las Vegas convention in summer 1997, the largest of these fantasy sports operators talked for the first time about joining forces. "It was supposed to be a consumer event for fantasy football," Wolf explains, "but not many showed up except for all of us who were running companies. So we got together and we were like, 'Wow, this is a shame that this hobby is not more popular.' We wondered what we could do to increase awareness of fantasy sports worldwide." The following year they met again and in 1999 created the Fantasy Sports Players Association (FSPA). As Wolf describes it, the fantasy industry was plagued by "turmoil, strife, confusion, misinformation, politics, and a lack of education."

For a few years the FSPA wasn't gaining much traction; indeed, the NFL Players Association objected to the word "Players" in the fantasy group's name and threatened to find a way to shut it down. So the name became Fantasy Sports Trade Association (FSTA).

Meanwhile, ESPN's SportsCenter, which had its debut back in 1979 but exploded in popularity in the 1990s, fed the growing fantasy fever by highlighting the very plays that interested fantasy gamers: long touchdown passes, interceptions returned for scores and game-winning field goals.

In 2000, the executive team at CBS SportsLine sought to place its software and suite of fantasy sports products on official league sites. The label "Official Fantasy Provider of the NFL" was enormously valuable and CBS SportsLine reportedly paid the NFL nearly $10 million for the rights.

"It was funny how quickly it tipped," Bruce Taylor recalls, "because for a long time the NFL considered fantasy football to be the enemy. They really hated us. And they hated people who played fantasy football. It took them a long time to figure out that the fantasy guys were their most voracious consumers, and the most anxious to pay them more money to watch more games on television. They just considered us a nuisance — and they thought fantasy football was gambling."

INSIDE FANTASY FOOTBALL /79

CHAPTER 5

The Daily Difference

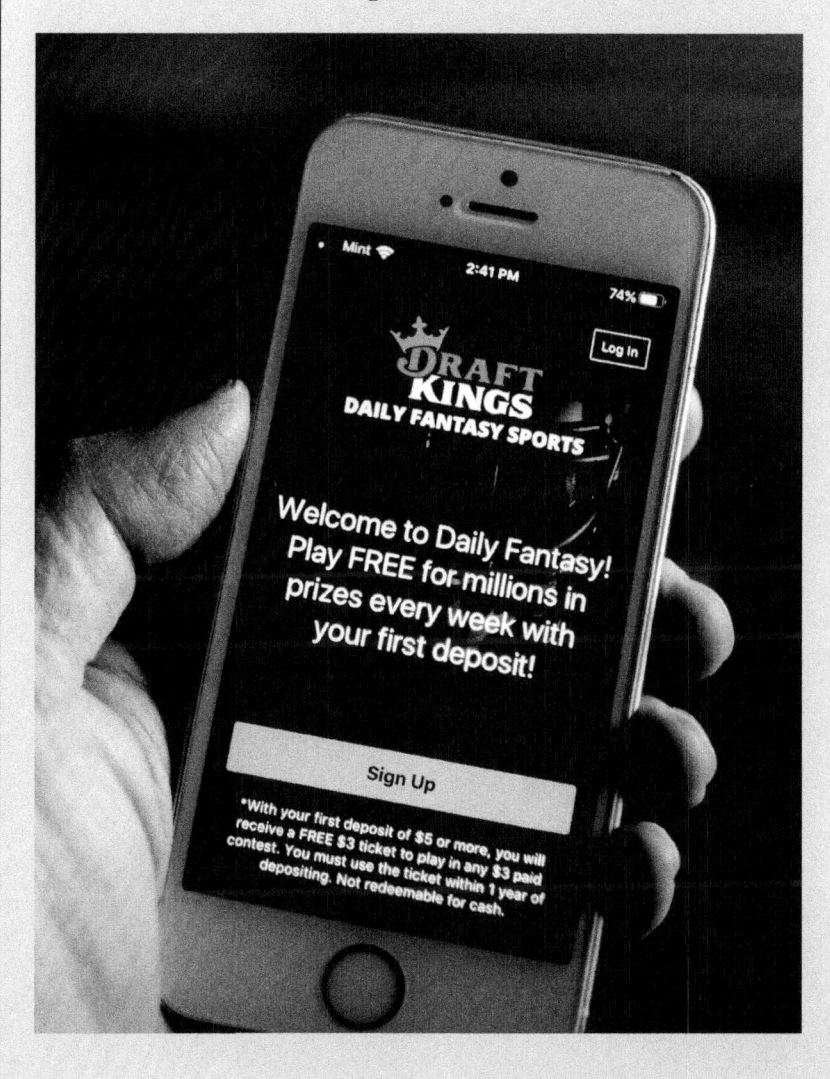

As the 1985 NFL season got underway, visitors to the Frontier Hotel and Casino in Las Vegas learned of a new type of game dubbed "Dream Team Football." For a $5 wager, gamblers selected their own squad for the current week's NFL slate, consisting of three quarterbacks, five running backs, six receivers and two kickers. Results, based on performances in NFL games, were posted each Tuesday, with $2,000 to the winner. (Trivia: the casino launched the Vegas career of Elvis Presley, who performed his first live show there in April 1956.)

Cliff Charpentier wrote in *Fantasy Football Digest* at the time, "As an avid Fantasy Football participant, I find the dream team concept — matching my drafting skills and luck against hundreds or thousands of other fantasy players — very exciting. Next time I'm in Las Vegas during the football season, you can be sure to find me entering a team or two in Frontier's Dream Team Contest."

It's fitting that the daily form of fantasy sports (DFS) originated at a casino rather than in, say, a basement like Bill Winkenbach's in Oakland, because the daily game has more in common with sports gambling than does traditional fantasy football. Indeed, Daniel Wallach, a gaming industry attorney, says, "Fantasy sports was traditionally a season-long contest that was something common among coworkers, friends and family. In the season-long contests, you're devoting hours upon hours each week and you have to wait until the end of the season to find out who won. The gratification doesn't get any more instant than in daily fantasy sports. You have an outcome every single day, and if you don't like your lineup today and you lost, you get to start over again tomorrow."

Despite the intrigue of daily fantasy in Vegas in the mid-80s, it took years for the DFS format to become a national obsession. The breakthrough was made possible by an act of Congress — one that was actually designed to limit gambling. The bill was called "The Unlawful Internet Gambling Enforcement Act" of 2006, which was supposed to curb gambling by blocking credit card payments for bets. Its sponsor in the House, Iowa Republican Jim Leach, said online gambling "serves no social purpose" and is "crack cocaine for gamblers." The NFL was among the measure's strongest supporters.

Indeed, 15 years earlier NFL commissioner Paul Tagliabue testified on Capitol Hill about players being influenced by gamblers. "We have to draw a line between sports and gambling. If we break the line down, and if we have the state sanctioning gambling, then I think we run a very serious risk that the athlete, whether he's young or old, will say it doesn't really matter. If I can do it at the 7-11, if I can do it at the pharmacy, if I can do it at the grocery store, why not take the $50 [as an inducement from gamblers] that's offered in the summer camp?"

But the bill Leach authored specifically exempted fantasy sports, as long as they were dependent more on skill than chance. Later, Leach conceded that he and his colleagues had no clue about the Pandora's box they opened. "The daily idea of fantasy sports was not conceived of when the bill was passed," he said.

The legislation provided a detailed description of what constitutes a "bet" or "wager," but then carved out this critically important exemption:

> (ix) participation in any fantasy or simulation sports game or educational game or contest in which (if the game or contest involves a team or teams) no fantasy or simulation sports team is based on the current membership of an actual team that is a member of an amateur or professional sports organization (as those terms are defined in section 3701 of title 28) and that meets the following conditions:
>
> (I) All prizes and awards offered to winning participants are established and made known to the participants in advance of the game or contest and their value is not determined by the number of participants or the amount of any fees paid by those participants.
>
> (II) All winning outcomes reflect the relative knowledge and skill of the participants and are determined predominantly by accumulated statistical results of the performance of individuals (athletes in the case of sports events) in multiple real-world sporting or other events.
>
> (III) No winning outcome is based—
>
> (aa) on the score, point-spread, or any performance or performances of any single real-world team or any

combination of such teams; or

(bb) solely on any single performance of an individual athlete in any single real-world sporting or other event.

Entrepreneurs in the U.S. did not immediately identify the correlation between the exemption Congress had provided and the little known world of daily fantasy sports. However, marketers in the UK, some of whom had worked as online poker executives, were intrigued by the possibilities — noting that season-long fantasy leagues moved too slowly for younger enthusiasts eager for instant gratification.

In 2007, businessman Nigel Eccles and his colleagues in Scotland launched a prediction site called Hubdub on which users bet on the outcomes of real-life news events using virtual money. In what turned out to be a business flop and a logistical fiasco, Hubdub hired students from the University of Edinburgh to sit and watch news programming in order to tabulate the results of news predictions. The site quickly burned up its $1.2 million in financing. "The fatal flaw," Eccles conceded, "was that there wasn't really a business model. So even though we were getting the scale in users, we just couldn't figure out how we would turn it into an interesting business."

Undaunted, Eccles' group turned to a sports-themed fantasy game in 2009 in which players could win money by drafting a baseball lineup to compete against anonymous online opponents. They called it FanDuel.

Meanwhile, across the pond near Boston three young entrepreneurs working at Vistaprint, an internet marketing

FanDuel's founder Nigel Eccles.

company later renamed Cimpress, were also mulling the possibilities for daily fantasy sports. They were Jason Robins, a Duke graduate with degrees in economics and computer science; Matt Kalish, a Columbia grad and fantasy baseball fan, and Paul Liberman, a graduate of Worcester Polytechnic Institute in Massachusetts. Working in the spare bedroom of Liberman's town house in Watertown, Massachusetts, and strategizing during breaks at Boston Beer Works, they mapped out an online sports venture designed to package the excitement of a season-long fantasy league into a single day's competition. They called it DraftKings.

"Estimates are that there are something like 30 million fantasy sports players, and only about 50,000 of them have tried daily so far," Kalish told the *Boston Globe* at the time. "That's a huge opportunity." He and his partners made their pitch to nearly 50 potential investors, with no takers until Ryan Moore at Accomplice Ventures put in some money followed by Peter

DraftKings founders (l to r) Matt Kalish, Paul Liberman and Jason Robins, pictured in 2017.

Blacklow of Boston Seed and a few others to create a $1.4 million startup. "We found in daily fantasy sports that having user liquidity was a huge thing," Robins explained. "It was basically a marketplace as well as a game. We were matchmaking among people who wanted to play, so having a lot of users who were playing actively was really important and it created tremendous network effects along the way."

A few months later DraftKings hosted its first daily fantasy baseball contest, for which a few dozen family members and friends paid $20 per lineup and competed for a pot worth about $400. The company's profit was $40.

Circa 2010 there were as many as 15 startups competing in the uncharted DFS space. One, invented by Manhattan marketing men Brian Schwartz and Mark Nerenberg, was called DraftStreet, offering innovative snake drafts in DFS contests.

Another, known as StarStreet, allowed users to play head-to-head against other users by putting anywhere from $1 to $50 into a pool. "Let's say you want to put in $10," the founder, Jeremy Levine — who would later create Underdog Fantasy — told the *Globe*. "We add a 7 percent commission, so you're paying $10.70, but you have a chance to win $20." With this formula, Levine explained, "We've noticed people getting totally addicted, playing every night."

StarStreet was purchased by DraftKings and then closed down. Levine then founded a second daily fantasy site called DRAFT that was eventually purchased by Paddy Power Betfair, which then bought FanDuel, which then merged DRAFT into FanDuel.

Matt King, the head of Fanatics, Inc. and before that CEO at FanDuel, says of the period, "Fantasy was a market that was stagnant. The younger sports fans weren't engaging with fantasy, and so the insight was, what if we take the mechanics of research and competing and playing with your friends and put it in a format that is geared for a hard to reach but very important category of millennial 18-to-35 year olds. Let's make it mobile, faster, and see how that goes."

In January 2013 FanDuel closed an $11 million round of financing and welcomed Comcast Ventures as an investor. Getting the capital affiliate of Comcast Corporation to invest and become part of FanDuel's board added instant credibility to a company and industry that desperately needed it in order to grow. Later that year DraftKings announced $7 million in funding (a sum that grew to over $40 million within 12 months — including an investment from Major League Baseball).

Before long, both companies' executives concluded that the easiest way to attract customers was to offer enormous jackpots. In 2013 DraftKings awarded over $50 million in prizes. On Dec. 8 of that year, in the FanDuel Fantasy Football Championship, a Sioux City, Iowa, sales manager named Travis Spieth turned $10 into daily fantasy's first one-day millionaire prize. A year later, in the same contest, a Pasadena, California, personal trainer named Scott Hanson was crowned the first daily fantasy multimillionaire by winning the $2 million grand prize.

According to ESPN's research, DFS entry fees in the United States had jumped from $20 million in 2011 to $1 billion in 2014. That year DraftKings acquired StarStreet and DraftStreet, immediately expanding DraftKings' customer base by more than 50 percent.

"The DraftStreet acquisition enables us to offer the best daily fantasy sports games in the market with a superior customer experience," boasted Jason Robins.

"DraftKings and DraftStreet have long enjoyed a highly competitive, but friendly relationship," added Brian Schwartz. "We are thrilled to join the DraftKings family and believe that combining our offerings creates a major win for both companies, the daily fantasy sports industry, and most importantly, our players."

At that point, 16 of the 32 NFL teams had formal ties with either DraftKings or FanDuel. The following year DraftKings and FanDuel announced funding rounds totaling $575 million, making the two DFS giants each worth over $1 billion and, as the 2015 NFL season began, the largest advertisers in America.

Against that background, an October 6, 2015 story on the

front page of *The New York Times* under the headline, "Scandal in Unchecked World of Fantasy Sports," was a bombshell. The report explained that a DraftKings employee, Ethan Haskell, disclosed confidential data on how DFS players were constructing their lineups before the start of games in the third week of the NFL season. Haskell, it turned out, won $350,000 in DFS on the competing FanDuel site. "It is absolutely akin to insider trading," said Daniel Wallach, a sports and gambling lawyer at Becker & Poliakoff in Fort Lauderdale, Fla. "It gives that person a distinct edge in a contest." As *The Times* explained, "The episode has raised questions about who at daily fantasy companies has access to valuable data, such as which players a majority of the money is being bet on; how it is protected; and whether the industry can — or wants — to police itself."

"Are the contests fair?" asked Lester Holt on NBC. "It's a question dominating the sports world."

Jason Robins went before the media stating, "This incident was based on complete misrepresentation, and bad reporting frankly ... we found that there is absolutely no evidence of ethical wrongdoing."

It didn't sit well with bloggers and latenight hosts, among them Trevor Noah, who told viewers, "Online fantasy sports betting is an unregulated marketplace that seems to be screwing everyday Americans out of their hard-earned money."

Three weeks later at the Republican presidential debate in Boulder, Colorado, one of the moderators, Carl Quintanilla, asked Florida's Jeb Bush, "Governor Bush, daily fantasy sports has become a phenomenon in this country, will award billions of dollars in prize money this year. But to play you have to assess

Chris Christie at the GOP debate in Colorado in 2015.

your odds, put money at risk, wait for an outcome that's out of your control. Isn't that the definition of gambling, and should the Federal Government treat it as such?"

> BUSH: Well, first of all, I'm 7 and 0 in my fantasy league.
> QUINTANILLA: I had a feeling you were going to brag about that.
> BUSH: Gronkowski is still going strong. I have Ryan Tannehill, Marco, as my quarterback, he was 18 for 19 last week. So I'm doing great. But we're not gambling. And I think this has become something that needs to be looked at in terms of regulation. Effectively it is day trading without any regulation at all. And when you have insider

information, which apparently has been the case, where people use that information and use big data to try to take advantage of it, there has to be some regulation. If they can't regulate themselves, then the NFL needs to look at just, you know, moving away from them a little bit. And there should be some regulation. I have no clue whether the federal government is the proper place, my instinct is to say, hell no, just about everything about the federal government.

CHRIS CHRISTIE: Carl, are we really talking about getting government involved in fantasy football?

(LAUGHTER)

CHRISTIE: We have — wait a second, we have $19 trillion in debt. We have people out of work. We have ISIS and al-Qaeda attacking us. And we're talking about fantasy football? Can we stop?

(APPLAUSE)

CHRISTIE: How about this? How about we get the government to do what they're supposed to be doing, secure our borders, protect our people, and support American values and American families. Enough on fantasy football. Let people play, who cares?

Actually, Chris Christie cared a lot. In 2012 he had signed legislation in New Jersey to legalize sports betting, a measure designed to revitalize businesses in Atlantic City, whose once-bustling casinos were hurting. But the New Jersey act ran counter to a federal law that banned sports betting outside Nevada and a few other locations.

While the Jersey case inched its way through the courts, attorneys general in New York, Illinois, Texas, Mississippi, Hawaii and Nevada all determined that DFS violated their gambling laws. In 2016 FanDuel received this ominous warning from auditors at Deloitte:

"It is possible that the number of states where the state attorney general may issue opinions against the group's activities could expand and the group's activities could be determined to be unlawful in those states and therefore prohibited from operating.

"The potential for such an outcome represents a material uncertainty that casts significant doubt upon the group and the company's ability to continue as a going concern."

ESPN scrubbed a deal to invest multi-millions in DraftKings less than a year after announcing it.

It was a rugged time for fantasy sports. DFS games were getting shut down in many states and the industry was in what the head of the Fantasy Sports Trade Association, Paul Charchian, described to me as "a moment of chaos." A boost of confidence came in 2016 when "Shark Tank" billionaire Mark Cuban made an investment in Fantasy Labs, whose business plan was "providing daily fantasy sports players with the data, tools, and analytics necessary to compete at a high level in DFS."

Charchian arranged for Cuban to be the headline speaker at the FSTA's 2016 summer conference in Dallas, where Cuban resided as the high-profile owner of the NBA's Mavericks. "He came on stage and told the audience not to panic," recalls Charchian. "He said people loved to play fantasy and it was going to

Paul Charchian, left, and Mark Cuban at the FSTA's 2016 summer conference in Dallas.

ultimately prevail, which it did." (Four years later Cuban would become an investor in Underdog Fantasy.)

♦ ♦ ♦

In late 2017 DraftKings and FanDuel announced plans to merge, only to have the Federal Trade Commission object based on antitrust regulations. The merger was called off and daily fantasy sports again seemed to be in danger of total collapse.

But on May 14, 2018, everything changed. In the case growing out of Chris Christie's legislation from years earlier, the U.S. Supreme Court overturned the Professional and Amateur Sports Protection Act, the 1992 law which had effectively banned sports betting in most of America. "It is as if federal officers were installed in state legislative chambers and were armed with the authority to stop legislators from voting on any offending proposals," Justice Samuel A. Alito Jr. wrote for the majority. "A more direct affront to state sovereignty is not easy to imagine."

Alito said there were reasonable policy arguments on both sides about whether to legalize sports betting. "Supporters argue that legalization will produce revenue for the states and critically weaken illegal sports betting operations, which are often run by organized crime," he wrote. "Opponents contend that legalizing sports gambling will hook the young on gambling, encourage people of modest means to squander their savings and earnings, and corrupt professional and college sports." But the root question he said was whether Congress had crossed a constitutional line in forcing states to do its work.

The landmark ruling gave states the right to legalize sports gambling and opened the door even wider for daily fantasy gaming. "If sports betting was OK, then certainly fantasy sports is OK," said Greg Ambrosius, founder of the National Fantasy Football Championships, "and we have seen an almost 20 percent jump in participation in fantasy leagues."

The organization known for decades as the Fantasy Sports Trade Association abruptly changed its name to the Fantasy Sports and Gaming Association.

FanDuel and DraftKings were soon challenged by dozens of operators offering their own twists on DFS competition. But the two powerhouse companies had a major head start in lobbying with individual states, having already mobilized an army of former regulators and politicians to press for sports betting in state capitals.

DraftKings co-founder Jason Robins, who would attain billionaire status in 2021, noted that one of the NFL's primary objectives is getting people to care about every second of every game. Fantasy sports, whether traditional or daily, are "a great vehicle to do that," he said. But the NFL commissioner Roger Goodell emphasized, "We see a big distinction between seasonal fantasy and daily fantasy. I want to make sure there's proper consumer protection." Despite Goodell's stated intentions, adequately protecting consumers remains a longshot proposition.

Since the 2018 Supreme Court ruling, the lines separating fantasy gaming from outright sports gambling have become increasingly blurred. The NFL has embraced both. Many expert commentators have broadened their fantasy football offerings to include betting advice. Matthew Berry, whose fantasy football newsletter Fantasy Life is among the most popular, has added a companion newsletter Betting Life — and on some days it's difficult to distinguish the content of one from the other.

That raises questions about addiction for fantasy players, especially when it comes to DFS and pick'em contests. Million-dollar prize pools take the enticement for some participants far beyond what was envisioned back in the day at the King's X bar in Oakland.

CHAPTER 6

Major Media Get Hooked

The NFL's state-of-the-art television studio in Southern California.

In late 2007, with the Philadelphia Eagles clinging to a 10-6 lead over Dallas, Brian Westbrook broke free for what appeared to be a 25-yard touchdown. Instead of scoring, however, Westbrook dropped to the ground at the 1-yard line allowing the Eagles to run out the clock. It's a play that lives in fantasy football infamy, because while Westbrook's action didn't affect the real game — in fact, it cemented the Eagles victory — it created instant winners and losers among fantasy competitors. Had Westbrook crossed the goal line it would have been worth six fantasy points in standard scoring. Since then, NFL players, coaches and TV announcers have focused more pointedly about how the real game impacts the pretend game.

That same year ESPN hired Matthew Berry, who had begun to establish himself as a fantasy guru with the handle "The Talented Mr. Roto," to be its in-house fantasy football expert. "Up until that point, fantasy football had been relegated to this niche in the sort of back corners of the internet," Berry recalls. "It's nerdy, geeky, maybe it's gambling. The leagues held it at an arm's length. Athletes certainly looked upon it with disdain. I felt like there was real potential, because all of a sudden ESPN was willing to invest in fantasy football — they recognized how important it was to their fans."

During a five-year period beginning in 2007 the number of fantasy players more than doubled, according to research from the Fantasy Sports & Gaming Association. The NFL's Red Zone channel, aimed at the fantasy audience, had its debut in 2009. Programming specifically geared toward fantasy football increased and analysts like Berry dramatically expanded their audience.

In 2010, ESPN released a report showing that fantasy sport participants consumed nearly three times as much media as other sports fans. Meanwhile, in a survey of 1,400 online users, the NFL found that fantasy players watch two to three more hours of televised football each Sunday than fans with ordinary rooting interest. Fantasy football shows soon became among the most popular in sports media. ESPN launched a three-hour Sunday morning show. The NFL Network and Peacock have hourlong programs on weekdays. YouTube has numerous fantasy football shows as does SiriusXM radio.

By 2023, according to Comscore data (based on participation on mobile devices during October of that season), ESPN was the leading fantasy sports provider with roughly 12 million customers. Yahoo followed with 6 million. DraftKings had about 5 million (when combined with its sportsbook betting app), while FanDuel had just under 4 million combined customers. NFL.com was next with about 2.5 million users. Rounding out the top 10 were PrizePicks, Sleeper and Underdog, each at about 1 million. That's over 30 million people engaged with fantasy sports — almost all of it football — measured on mobile devices alone.

Among magazines displayed on a store rack in 2014 only two were not about fantasy football.

♦ ♦ ♦

The FX sitcom "The League," described by one critic as a prime example of "fantasy football hooliganism," depicted six friends competing in a fantasy football league. The series ran for seven seasons from 2009 to 2015 and featured frequent cameos from then-current and former NFL players, further establishing fantasy football's place in the zeitgeist.

In the premiere episode, a defense attorney trades his first-round draft pick to a prosecutor in order to knock three years off the prison sentence of a man who robbed liquor stores. Meanwhile, another league member practically kidnaps a 9-year-old boy known as "The Oracle" for his football prowess, and pumps him for advice. And the league's commissioner is threatened with divorce by his wife if he attends the draft party, which he attends, leading to their breakup. "God bless fantasy football," says the guy. "There are many things a man can do with his time. This is better than those things."

♦ ♦ ♦

While many media innovations have spurred the growth of fantasy football, perhaps the most effective has been "Sunday Ticket," launched by DirecTV in 1994 under contract with the NFL. The service allows subscribers to watch all out-of-town NFL games on Sunday that are not available in the customer's local broadcast feeds. In 2023 the deal moved to YouTube. The following year, in a stunning judgment, a federal jury in Los Angeles found the NFL liable in a suit over price-fixing, and ordered the league to pay $4.7 billion in damages — a sum that

"The League" on FX brought fantasy football to a mainstream audience for seven seasons.

could have tripled under federal antitrust laws. The class action applied to more than 2.4 million residential subscribers and 48,000 businesses, mostly bars and restaurants, that purchased "NFL Sunday Ticket" between 2011 and 2023.

The lawsuit was originally filed in 2015 by the Mucky Duck sports bar in San Francisco. In 2017 U.S. District Judge Beverly Reid O'Connell dismissed the suit and ruled for the NFL, saying "Sunday Ticket" did not reduce output of NFL games and that even though DirecTV might have charged inflated prices, that did not "on its own, constitute harm to competition" because it had to negotiate with the NFL to carry the games. Two years later, the 9th Circuit Court of Appeals reinstated the case. According to memos presented by attorneys for the plaintiffs, Fox and CBS have always wanted the league to charge premium prices for "Sunday Ticket" so that it doesn't eat into local ratings — the more subscribers to "Sunday Ticket" the greater the threat to local audience numbers. During opening statements, attorney Amanda Bonn showed a 2020 term sheet by Fox Sports demanding the NFL ensure "Sunday Ticket" would be priced above $293.96 per season. When the "Sunday Ticket" contract was up for bid in 2022, ESPN wanted to offer the package on its streaming service for $70 per season, along with offering a team-by-team product, according to an email shown in court. That was rejected by the NFL.

Just as the 2024 preseason was beginning, Judge Philip S. Gutierrez delivered a ruling even more stunning than the original finding: He dismissed the case, writing, "No reasonable jury could have found class-wide injury or damages."

♦ ♦ ♦

In addition to "Sunday Ticket," the media playing field for fantasy football has expanded along with fantasy football's popularity. In addition to network feeds, the NFL captures game action from two cameras positioned high above the field in every stadium. The "All-22" angle in these so-called coaches' tapes captures every player on the field in a single shot, and the "End Zone" camera provides a downfield view as the play unfolds. The league makes these resources available to fans through NFL Game Pass, in packages ranging in cost from $6.99 to $14.99 per month.

Fantasy football is so potent that the NFL operates its own platform, NFL Fantasy. The site offers detailed fantasy advice and products, with come-ons such as, "Crush the competition with tools that help you start your best lineup and improve your fantasy team!" The NFL's fantasy app includes a "premium" paid tier with additional content for those who play — which they can do directly on the NFL's platform.

Perhaps the most telling sign that the NFL has not only accepted fantasy football but allowed it to dominate its messaging is the roster of writers and podcasters — all NFL employees — who give tips and advice about players' ability and match-ups.

Marcas Grant was hired by the NFL in 2011 as a fantasy football writer. "They had just taken it in house," he told me, "because they realized they were missing a big revenue opportunity and a big content-driving opportunity. Within the first couple

Marcas Grant, left, with Michael Florio, hosting the NFL's own TV series about fantasy football.

of years I was there, I started to see it really grow. ... You know the old quote, 'sports is the toy department of life.' We were sort of the experimental wing toy department. We were the weird kids in the corner poring over our stats and trying to predict the future."

◆ ◆ ◆

The NFL's more recent media expansion has been most notable on streaming outlets, with games on Amazon Prime, Peacock and, in 2024, on Christmas Day via the giant Netflix platform, reaching 300 million customers worldwide. The league collected $150 million from Netflix for the Christmas doubleheader, featuring the Kansas City Chiefs at Pittsburgh Steelers and the Baltimore Ravens at Houston Texans.

"All of the streaming platforms have allowed us to reach a younger average audience age," Commissioner Roger Goodell said in announcing the Netflix deal. "There are several people who are fans of the NFL who aren't on pay systems anymore because they are changing. People are leaving in some cases, but we're still committed to those platforms. Our job is to be everywhere our fans are. ... For us to be the first sport that Netflix is invested in to bring to their subscribers, I think is a statement about our content and the potential opportunity between the two."

Netflix has been playing ball with the NFL since launching the hit series "Quarterback" in 2023, followed in '24 by "Receiver," featuring five top pass catchers on and off the field: Davante Adams (Raiders), Justin Jefferson (Vikings), George Kittle and Deebo Samuel (49ers), and Amon-Ra St. Brown (Lions).

"Last year, we decided to take a big bet on live — tapping into massive fandoms across comedy, reality TV, sports, and more," said Netflix Chief Content Officer Bela Bajaria. "There are no live annual events, sports or otherwise, that compare with the audiences NFL football attracts. We're so excited that the NFL's Christmas Day games will be only on Netflix."

The Netflix distribution is important as part of the NFL's plan for growing the game internationally. "We are obviously focused on becoming more global," Goodell said. "So that's a huge benefit to us." The list of foreign venues includes England, Germany, Mexico, Brazil and, in 2025, Spain.

"It's a reflection of the changing media landscape," Goodell added. "The reality is, it's changing before our eyes."

As *USA Today's* veteran reporter Jarrett Bell put it in summarizing the NFL's media expansion, "Goodell is quite the prophet. As in profit."

CHAPTER 7

Best Ball . . . Mania

In January, 2024 best ball drafters were already picking Sam LaPorta of the Lions as TE1.

It was a Tuesday in January, 2023, two days after the conference championship games and nearly two weeks before the Chiefs would meet the 49ers in Super Bowl LVIII to conclude the NFL season. What happened that day was described by Matthew Berry as certain to appeal to "fantasy football sickos of all shapes and sizes." Underdog Fantasy kicked off its best ball tournaments for the *following* season — fully 220 days before the Chiefs would host the Ravens to begin the 2024 campaign. That day "The Big Board" featured $2 million in prize money ($200,000 to first place) for a $10 entry fee, while "The Little Board" offered $150,000 in prizes ($15,000 to the top winner) for a $3 entry fee.

These offerings by Underdog confirmed two things that legions of sickos know well: Fantasy football is now played year-long, not just in-season, and the format making it possible, best ball, is soaring in popularity.

A few months later, just two days after the NFL draft, Underdog went all in with its flagship contest, "Best Ball Mania." The game was open to 672,700 entries (up to 150 per person), each paying $25 (a $16.8 million take) with $15 million in prizes, including $1.5 million for first place. This prompted

Berry's colleague Peter Overzet, the podcaster and writer, to declare, "We made it. Our long national nightmare is over. Best Ball Mania V is finally here. It's Best Ball Christmas!"

If you think of season-long fantasy football as a cupcake, then for many participants the draft is the icing — and who among us hasn't ever licked the icing and tossed away the cake? Even the inventors of fantasy football, the GOPPPL crew in Oakland, referred to their entire game as "The Draft."

In best ball, participants draft a team of NFL players but unlike in traditional leagues or DFS, there are no in-season roster moves — in fact, there's nothing for the entrant to do following the draft but sit and wait. This means no trades, no waiver wire pickups and no setting lineups. The platform's computer automatically selects each week's highest-scoring players after the fact to determine your most successful lineup each week. Best ball contests are available in various configurations from Underdog, Yahoo, DraftKings, FanDuel and other providers, making best ball the fast-growing segment of fantasy football.

"You have to give a lot of credit to Underdog," said Berry, who is an investor in the company. "They built a great product, with the ability to do it so easily and quickly. I think that's one of the reasons it has grown in the way it has."

"The NFL has created more of a year-long fan," Overzet added. "People are thinking about their fantasy teams earlier and earlier and best ball provides this vehicle for people to draft without actually having to manage it in season, which is the rub because anyone who's ever managed more than a handful of leagues hates themselves by week five when they're having to deal with all the waivers and the starts and the sits. So yep, best ball filled this void for people who love to draft and love talking about this year round, but don't have the time to manage all of those leagues."

Bob Lung, the creator of Fantasy Football Expo, told me, "Best ball is basically the gateway drug to being in way too many leagues. It's really a pacifier for those in the offseason who can't make it to August to draft. And they're giving away big money. Best ball is just another lottery."

♦ ♦ ♦

According to one view of history, CDM Sports developed this type of format in 1997 with its "Draft & Play" series for newspapers and the internet. Readers drafted players and did nothing else but watch the games to see how they were doing.

Meanwhile, Emil Kadlec, the acclaimed fantasy pioneer and historian, was cooking up what was an early, perhaps the first, actual best ball league. He and his colleagues at Fan Ex (short for "Fantasy Experts") were doing mid-summer preparation for regular drafts in 1998 and decided to try a new form of draft practice. Kadlec told the group: "Let's do a regular meaningful draft (league) and have no free agency or any lineups each week of the NFL season. We can have Terry Canon, the commissioner, pick our best lineups from our rosters each week on Tuesday morning after all the week's games are completed. This way each manager does not have to do any additional work and the league is legit." The group agreed and launched the "Fantasy Analysis Draft" league (FAD).

Kadlec, using the team name "Candy Bones," won the inaugural 12-team competition. His roster was led by the sea-

In 2018, Emil Kadlec, right, entered the Fantasy Football World Championships' Hall of Fame, receiving his award from founder Ian Ritchie.

son's MVP, running back Terrell Davis, who amassed 2,008 rushing yards and an additional 217 receiving yards for the Denver Broncos. (For the record, Commissioner Canon finished in last place.)

Kadlec grew up in Albuquerque and earned a master's in electrical engineering while discovering a love for fantasy football. He formed a league at work which he called The Watermelon Pro Football League, named after the Sandia Mountains ("watermelon" in Spanish).

As for the term "best ball," it was coined by MyFantasyLeague.com — making reference to the format in golf where partners select the best ball after each shot, and then both hit from that spot. The format exploded in 2020 during the pandemic, primarily on Underdog, founded that same year by Jeremy Levine. Among his backers were several notable investors

UNDERDOG FANTASY

Made possible by:

MARK CUBAN

ADAM SCHEFTER · MATTHEW DELLAVEDOVA

JEREMY LEVINE · BRANDON STAKENBORG

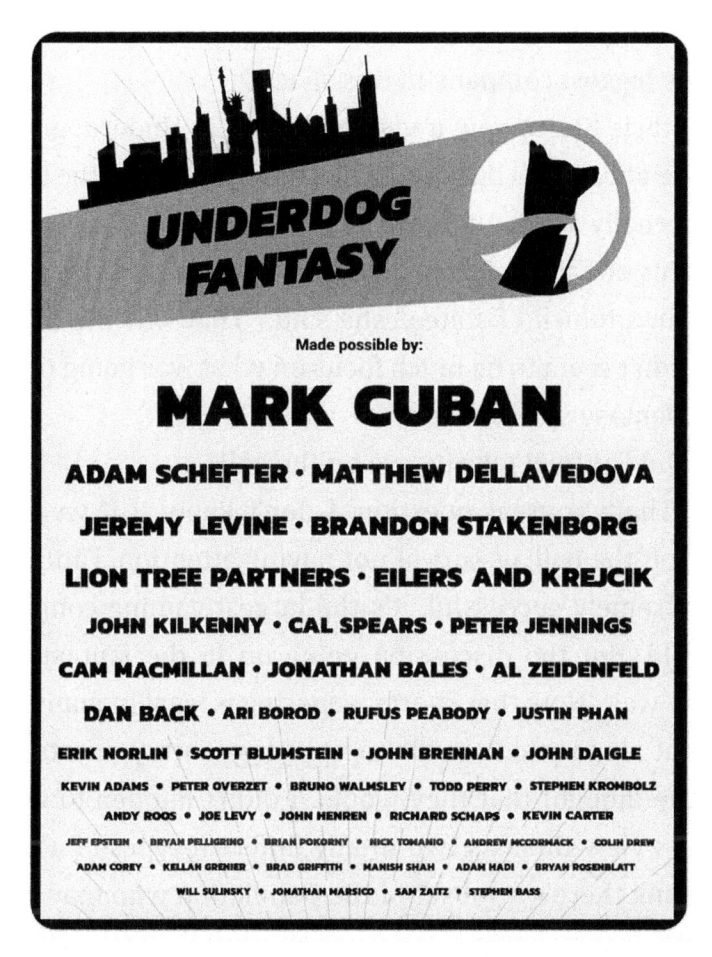

LION TREE PARTNERS · EILERS AND KREJCIK

JOHN KILKENNY · CAL SPEARS · PETER JENNINGS

CAM MACMILLAN · JONATHAN BALES · AL ZEIDENFELD

DAN BACK · ARI BOROD · RUFUS PEABODY · JUSTIN PHAN

ERIK NORLIN · SCOTT BLUMSTEIN · JOHN BRENNAN · JOHN DAIGLE

KEVIN ADAMS · PETER OVERZET · BRUNO WALMSLEY · TODD PERRY · STEPHEN KROMBOLZ

ANDY ROOS · JOE LEVY · JOHN HENREN · RICHARD SCHAPS · KEVIN CARTER

JEFF EPSTEIN · BRYAN PELLIGRINO · BRIAN POKORNY · NICK TOMANIO · ANDREW MCCORMACK · COLIN DREW

ADAM COREY · KELLAN GRENIER · BRAD GRIFFITH · MANISH SHAH · ADAM HADI · BRYAN ROSENBLATT

WILL SULINSKY · JONATHAN MARSICO · SAM ZAITZ · STEPHEN BASS

Underdog's original investors weren't nobodies.

including a group headed by "Shark Tank" billionaire Mark Cuban along with ESPN's Adam Schefter, and joined later by NBA star Kevin Durant, Lions quarterback Jared Goff and Matthew Berry. "We were in a space with not a lot of product innovation," Levine explained, "and I thought there was more we could do for the American sports fan with a different customer experience. The opportunity at Underdog was to build out that vision in fantasy and in sports gaming as a whole. And we believed from the beginning that if we could build the best products, we could build the biggest company in this space."

Stacie Stern, now a vice president at Underdog, was an executive at FanDuel back in 2020. I asked her what the reaction was internally when Underdog's best ball made its big splash. "The focus at FanDuel was, quite honestly, on launching sports betting in a bunch of states," she said. "That was the mandate. There didn't seem to be much focus on what was going on in the outside fantasy sports world."

Did FanDuel take its eye off the ball?

"That's a great question. I don't know if it was taking the eye off the ball, or sort of not paying attention. FanDuel has been extremely successful, it's the largest gaming company in the world. But the discussion going on in the fantasy sports industry was, 'Now that sports wagering is legal in many states, does that mean people will stop playing fantasy sports?' A lot of people thought that they would. I didn't happen to think so because I view them as two totally different types of activities. I also think there's a subset of the population who may not feel comfortable with betting and wagering, but they're comfortable with fantasy sports because it's skill and analysis and research, not that sports wagering isn't, but I think as soon as you flip it over to betting or gambling it makes some people nervous."

Best ball provides multiple benefits for both operators and the public. As noted, many participants enjoy the draft so much that it's appealing to play a game that's 100 percent drafting. The delayed outcome — you don't know how you fared until many months later — makes it easier to discount the risk (and fear) about losing money. Most importantly, best ball is played all year long, which is a major plus for fans as well as for companies operating fantasy football platforms.

Of course, there is another side. With guaranteed contests, such as Best Ball Mania, the operator is on the hook for the full prize payout, even if the contest doesn't fill. The day in September 2022 when BBM3 hit its mark of 451,200 participants, there was a raucous champagne celebration at Underdog's New York headquarters. The company's vice president, David Gamboa, posted: "3 years ago we sweated filling a $1 million prize pool tournament. Today we're filling a $10 million tournament a whole day early. Surreal stuff."

The major plus for operators is the windfall that comes by holding the money for as long as a year before making payouts. Industry veteran Paul Charchian knows a lot about the value of fantasy money. Among his many innovations is a company he

The staff celebration at Underdog when BBM3 hit its goal in 2022.

founded in 2008 called League Safe, which essentially holds the money for private fantasy leagues. He's a fan of best ball, noting, "If you said ten years ago, there's some format where people are gonna have 1,000 fantasy teams, I'd say that's impossible. How can you possibly do that? So yeah, I think it's great and from a business standpoint, the beauty of it is you get income coming on football when you never used to, from February into June."

♦ ♦ ♦

Underdog's rapid growth has contributed to a bitter, high-stakes battle being waged over another type of game known as pick'em, which Underdog has aggressively promoted. It's a form of parlay wagering in which players pick two or more "propositions" — for instance: Will Patrick Mahomes throw for over 275 yards this week and will Josh Jacobs score two or more touchdowns? But even the terminology in the previous two sentences is contentious, because some say pick'em is a form of gambling, while others insist it's another way to play fantasy football.

"FanDuel and DraftKings have spent hundreds of millions of dollars across all the states to buy lawmakers cigars and whiskey," Rick Wolf of the FSGA told me, to get them to declare that pick'em games are gambling and not fantasy. Underdog and PrizePicks are lobbying to keep these contests under the fantasy umbrella so they are governed by fantasy regulations.

Florida became an early hotbed in the fight when the state gaming commission ordered Underdog and PrizePicks to cease "offering or accepting illegal bets or wagers from residents," specifically citing pick'em style contests.

Underdog's argument boils down to this:

If you want to risk, say, $10 on whether Christian McCaffrey will score more than 2.5 touchdowns Sunday afternoon, that's a sports bet. But if you put up $10 on whether McCaffrey and Saquon Barkley each get more than 2.5 TDs, that's a fantasy contest. To many — including FanDuel and DraftKings — it's a distinction without a difference.

Underdog's Stacie Stern maintains, "It's enough of a roster for it to be a game of skill. So, depending on the state law, that varies and, yes, two players certainly may be a roster."

In attempting to mediate this multimillion-dollar matter, the FSGA suggests that such games be required to have at least five legs of a parlay proposition, covering different players on different teams. "I'm trying to educate both the industry and the regulators," said Wolf, "to make a decision that it is fantasy sports, because it's safer that way. We won't have a Jontay Porter case where somebody can put $80,000 on one guy, right? (Porter, the Toronto Raptors forward, was banned for life by the NBA after a league probe found he disclosed confidential information to sports bettors and wagered on games, even betting on the Raptors to lose.) And you're not going to compromise five guys from different teams in different locations. It's just not possible. It's safer for everyone that way. When it's players, you play on a fantasy site, when it's teams and everything else, you bet on it."

◆ ◆ ◆

As 2024 began, Underdog crowned Farid Shaheed its winner of BBM4 and wrote him a check for $3 million. That might stand as the biggest payout ever, since Underdog adjusted its prize pool for BBM5, with the top prize reduced to $1.5 million. Shaheed relied on a Green Bay Packer stack that included quarterback Jordan Love (28.44) and receiver Jayden Reed (23.9). His roster was highlighted by chalky Dallas receiver CeeDee Lamb, who smashed with 33.7.

Shaheed, 32, had a background playing poker but was only in his third year with best ball at the time of his win. "Stunned," he quit his job driving a semi and bought a Doberman puppy and a pickup truck. "I'm not going to claim to be some kind of wizard," he conceded. "I just got really lucky."

Meanwhile, from a media perspective, Underdog's phenomenal success has made an impression on its competitors. "I can't say enough good things about the way best ball has taken off over the last two or three years," Yahoo's Andy Behrens told me. "It's a function of the strength of the community and some of the analysts who enter that space. Underdog has done such a great job not only building great contests, but man, they've hired the right people and they've produced such good content. All of their content people you can tell are football geeks. I think some of the content around best ball is some of the best stuff that's getting produced in the fantasy space."

Adam Levitan, the outspoken fantasy football host and co-creator of the Establish the Run site, says "I'm too old now to be grinding the waiver wire and trades and all that, but I still love to draft. I think a lot of people feel that way. The draft is the absolute stone-cold best. ... I'll do it late at night lying in bed after my wife goes to sleep." An accomplished poker player, Levitan notes that best ball is "an established money maker. You

Because best ball starts so early, drafters can get caught by changes. Stefon Diggs was with the Bills until three months into the best ball season when he was traded to the Texans.

can get a ton of teams and there's a lot of strategy around it. I'm not surprised that it's insanely popular."

◆ ◆ ◆

Among the most prolific pundits in the best ball arena is Mason Dodd, who began live-streaming best ball drafts while at the University of Texas. After graduating in 2021 he expanded his Flock Fantasy business, operating from his home in Austin, and now takes his more than 200,000 YouTube subscribers on nightly trips across a live Underdog draft board — interspersing commentary, tips and analysis while explaining his own draft selections. He manages to conduct several hundred such drafts each year, with 2022 being his best personal season, achieving $150,000 in Underdog winnings.

[Trivia: Dodd's girlfriend is Haley Welch, who had a meteoric rise on social media as the "Hawk Tuah Girl," after making a quip about spitting during sex.]

"I probably work 80 hours a week during football season," Dodd explains, "live streaming at least 200 days in a row. But it's fantasy football — it's not a man's job or anything, it's a boy's job."

♦ ♦ ♦

Back in March 2020, David Gamboa sat at his desk with a laptop and a sketchbook, mulling Underdog's launch and the odds that best ball would be a game changer. "The world is shutting down," he wrote, referring to the pandemic, "and I'm sitting here sketching out the draft room and our logo. Working on only a dream that this might turn into something eventually."

Underdog founder Jeremy Levine called best ball his favorite part of the service. "When you ask people their favorite part of fantasy, sometimes they say winning. That's a good answer for those who win, but most often it's the draft. ... Casual customers love it, because they get to do the draft, and that's it. They don't have to worry about the management. But hardcore players also love it because they can do thousands. Our top customer in the 2022 season did over 4,000 real money, best

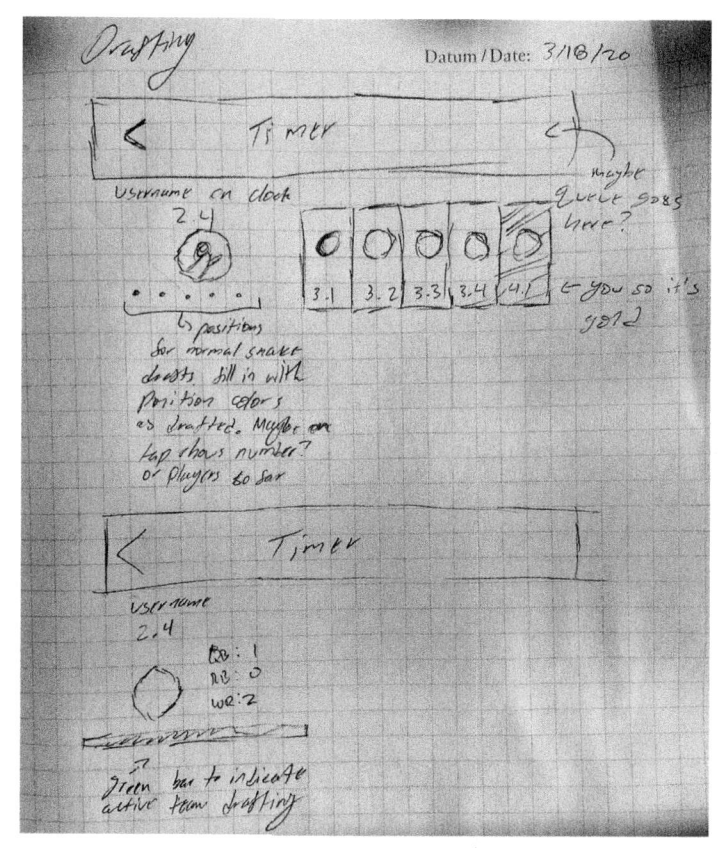

David Gamboa's original sketch in 2020, as he designed what is now the familiar Underdog draft screen.

ball drafts. ... It's a game that we really popularized, we actually launched about a month before FanDuel and DraftKings launched their best ball products."

On July 17, 2020, when Levine's company started best ball, it used the tagline:

Underdog. Made by people who love to draft.

CHAPTER 8
Top Talking Touts

Matthew Berry brings his "love and hate" to Peacock and other NBC platforms.

If you're among the roughly six million people who draft on Yahoo's popular platform prior to each NFL season, you know what it's like in those tense minutes leading up to the first pick, when the computer randomly assigns your draft position and the seasonal sweat kicks in. As you study the screen, a cheerful guy named Andy pops up with a video pep talk. If, for instance, you had the #1 pick in 2023, Andy said:

"First pick! Look at you! ... You shouldn't need me to tell you that historically this spot performs really well. ... At the top of the draft, you control the board. ... I'd wish you luck, but clearly you already have plenty of it."

If, on the other hand, you had the #8 pick:

"The great thing about the eighth pick is that you're definitely getting one of your eight favorite players in the draft. Hey, it could be worse. I'm not going to try and tell you that the eighth pick was a winning spot last year. What I can tell you is when I find myself in this spot, I like doubling up on a position in the first two rounds (two RBs or two WRs). One of my guiding principles in any draft is to be sure that I have a clear edge somewhere when it's all done."

Maybe you got the league's final slot:

"Twelfth and last pick in the draft, huh? Some people really like these turn picks. Here's hoping you're one of those weirdos because historically across decades and many thousands of Yahoo leagues, it's a little bit better to be in the top half of the draft. ... The turn is a great place to try some stuff. Perhaps to operate outside your RB-heavy comfort zone. This is a prime spot to go zero-RB. ... Maybe you're the person who triggers the quarterback run in round three or four. ... At the turn you have a great chance to control the board and, occasionally, to get people panicking."

The words of encouragement come from Andy Behrens, a fixture in Yahoo's fantasy operation since 2007, who records his Draft Slot Videos about six weeks before the start of each NFL season. "There's only certain times of year where anybody will recognize me in public," he notes. "But man, when it's the peak couple of weeks of football draft season, I get a lot of looks where people will kind of squint and ask, 'Hey, did we used to work together?' And I'll be, 'Like to play fantasy football?' And they're like, 'Oh, man!'"

What do fans tell you about their drafts?

"I find it funny that there are plenty of people out there who year after year say, 'I want those turn picks. Let me pick 12 and 13, or 10 and 11.' Well, we have years of data that suggests that is not where you want to be. I mean, the funny thing about drafts is they're not entirely fair."

Growing up in Chicago, where he still makes his home, Behrens' dad was a high school basketball coach, but his earliest sports memories involve Walter Payton, the Bears Hall of Fame running back who played from 1975 to '87. "I learned of fantasy football in college where I had a group of friends that were football obsessed. We heard the phrase 'fantasy football'

Yahoo's voice of encouragement Andy Behrens.

but knew little about it. We designed a league that was a spectacular failure, because it was way too complicated — we had every position, offense and defense." After college Behrens did some freelance sportswriting, which led to a gig at ESPN.com and then a job offer from Yahoo.

He also serves as president of the Fantasy Sports Writers Association, created in 2004. "It was a time," Behrens recalls, "when fantasy wasn't taken all that seriously, even by the major platforms that hosted games. It was kind of off in a corner and you couldn't possibly mix fantasy content with mainstream sports content, because this is nerd stuff over here and this is cool stuff over here. Then slowly people began to realize that if they played in one or two fantasy leagues they'll know the entire NFL and be a better informed fan. I think the fantasy experience and general sports fan experience have merged so that it's fair to say if you're not playing in a fantasy league you're not really a hardcore sports fan. All the major platforms are now giving fantasy airtime."

◆ ◆ ◆

You could probably write an entire book about fantasy football's top tout, Matthew Berry, except that he's already written it about himself: the 2013 best-selling memoir "Fantasy Life." Never at a loss for words, Berry used a bunch of them to describe the game:

"Fantasy sports is outrageous, poignant, obsessive, heartwarming, heartbreaking, frustrating, crazy, uplifting, life-changing, monstrously fun, very addicting, and, quite simply, the best thing ever invented."

Fantasy football's remarkable growth has led to a commensurate increase in the roster of experts, both established and wannabe. With so much time between weekly games, and considering the range of fantasy options — redraft, dynasty, DFS, best ball, pick'em and others — the thirst among participants for insider info is enormous. On YouTube alone, our researchers counted over 600 channels giving fantasy football advice.

Born in Denver in 1969, Matthew Berry's family relocated to five different cities by the time he was 13, winding up in Texas, where he self-described as "socially awkward," with "big, frizzy hair and thick glasses." He got his degree in electronic media from Syracuse University and became a comedy writer in Hollywood, landing a job with the famously low brow sitcom "Married... with Children." Already a fantasy sports buff, he picked up the phone one Saturday night in 2001 and called Steve

Mason's nationally-syndicated radio show, identifying himself as "Matthew in the Valley." As Mason recalls:

"He knew more about fantasy football than me, which is humbling for a know-it-all sports talk radio host. We spoke during the week. Matthew asked, 'Can I come in studio to do a fantasy football segment?' It had not really occurred to me, but I thought 'What the hell. I'm going to give this guy a shot.' He went from knowledgeable caller to dispensing fantasy football advice on the radio for a national audience in only seven days. For me, it was a really good segment. For Matthew, it was the beginning

Berry's 2013 book helped catapult him to the top of fantasy football's most renowned observers.

of his career as the Talented Mr. Roto, and, ultimately, his fantasy sports empire."

In his book, Berry recounts his moniker's origin story. "I wanted to be known as 'The Roto Whore,' because it was funny," he writes. His bosses hated it. "I told my wife that I wanted something that would make me seem like an expert but not one who took himself too seriously." He considered "Mr. Roto," "The Lord of Roto," "The Roto King" and "The Czar of Roto," but concluded they were all "brutal." After seeing the Matt Damon movie, "The Talented Mr. Ripley," he settled on "The Talented Mr. Roto and, "The silly, over-the-top name caught on."

Brandon Funston, the acclaimed fantasy writer who spent eight years at ESPN, 13 years at Yahoo and six years at *The Athletic*, recalls his first encounter with Berry. "He came to Yahoo looking for a job. The management thought he was too blue, too raunchy, pushing the envelope of what is PG-13 or less."

Berry took a gig at the fantasy site RotoWorld.com. Rick Wolf, who became his boss in 2002, recounted for me, "Because he was a Hollywood guy, he could write great fiction. He would make up stories. It'd be something like, 'Hey, I'm walking down the street. I bumped into J.Lo.' And he would make up a fantasy story about him talking to J.Lo.

"I found his articles to be the most entertaining out there. But we had a partnership with Fox Sports and they thought that some of the fantastic pop culture stuff that he was weaving within his articles was, you know, not what they wanted to publish on their site. Eventually we had to part ways, and he went and started his own site, TalentedMrRoto, and then sold that to ESPN. And once that happened, he and his team broke through with relentless energy. He's a fantastic entrepreneur and knows how to run multiple fantasy sports businesses."

Berry spent 15 years at ESPN (2007-2022) as the lead fantasy football expert, hosting "The Fantasy Show," ESPN's first daily program devoted to fantasy sports, and the Sunday morning staple "Fantasy Football Now." He says his first year at ESPN "was among the toughest of my life." He wasn't prepared for the intense feedback on social media about his style. "I was and always have been different from other fantasy analysts, but many people felt someone on ESPN should be just the stats and nothing else." But Berry had always injected humor and personal references in his writing, going all the way back to his days at Syracuse University. It probably didn't help that, "I have this very Jewy voice, and I can say that because I'm Jewish."

He jumped to NBC Sports in 2022, where he regularly appears on "Football Night in America" and hosts "Fantasy Football Happy Hour" weekdays on Peacock. He also operates his own "Fantasy Life" site and newsletter — the free version of which is distributed to over 400,000 subscribers — and expanded it to include "Betting Life" with the mission statement: "Fantasy football and sports betting for all, anytime, anywhere."

Berry's roster of superstar investors is remarkable. It includes basketball great LeBron James, singer John Legend, YouTube's co-founder Chad Hurley, Jacksonville Jaguars owner (with his father) Tony Khan, and the head of the Los Angeles Olympic Committee Casey Wasserman. "I had one rule in building the company," Berry says, "no assholes. I am too old and too successful to have to deal with assholes. I have managed to get myself to a place in life where I no longer have to deal with assholes. I can sorta do what I want."

He notes proudly that when he made the move from ESPN to NBC the news trended on Twitter with an outpouring of encouragement. "I got over 50,000 likes and thousands of comments, and kind thing after kind thing. It made me blush, the outpouring of love and support. As I said to my wife, 'Boy, it's nice to be trending on Twitter and not be dead or canceled.'"

One of Berry's most popular offerings is his long-running "Love/Hate" column, which showcases not only his insight into fantasy football rankings but also his passion for waxing about, well, almost anything — the type of stuff the execs at Fox didn't care for. For example, his first column for the 2023 NFL season began:

"It's noon on Peacock, but it's five o'clock somewhere!"

That's how I opened my very first show for NBC as I raised a glass and welcomed viewers to the bar where Fantasy Football Happy Hour is broadcast from. The show had originally been conceived to air in the late afternoon, hence the "happy hour" theme and setting. Somewhere between show creation and first air date the initial time slot changed, moving us to live at noon, however the idea of the show — buddies drinking at a bar and b.s.-ing about fantasy football and sports betting — remained the same.

So, in trying to solve the puzzle of how to explain why a lunch time show had a late afternoon name, I did what I have often done over the last 30 or so years.

I turned to Jimmy Buffett for inspiration.

Jimmy, of course, had a big hit with Alan Jackson on their song "It's Five O'Clock Somewhere," explaining that he really needed a drink after getting yelled at by his boss, even though "it's only half past twelve but I don't care... it's five o'clock somewhere."

I'm smiling as I write that last sentence.

Because, as any good Parrothead knows, it's always five o'clock in Margaritaville.

And anyone that has ever read or listened to me knows I am a massive Jimmy Buffett fan.

And as the world knows, we lost Jimmy this past weekend when his family announced he had passed away peacefully on the night of September 1, "surrounded by his family, friends, music and dogs."

I say that's how Berry's column *began*, because he wrote a total of 3,148 words about Buffett and attending concerts and all sorts of musings such as, "Who doesn't love going to the beach, basking in the sun, enjoying a cold drink as you watch the waves?" Finally, he gets around to the fantasy football stuff after quoting Buffett: "If life gives you limes, make margaritas."

That's Matthew Berry. Football fans either love him or hate him — and, for the most part, it's the former.

"I've had a truly blessed career and I've been given a great opportunity, which is my platform. I was lucky enough to get a job at ESPN, and I was lucky enough to have the people at ESPN listen to me when I said, 'There's this thing called fantasy football that's really fun and we should try to promote it. Now I'm on 'Football Night in America,' which is the highest rated TV show. So I'm lucky."

◆ ◆ ◆

Stephania Bell, Field Yates and Matthew Berry on ESPN before Berry moved to NBC and Peacock.

When Berry left ESPN the lead fantasy role went to Field Minister Yates, who, since he looks younger than his years while Berry looks older than his, seemed like he might have been The Talented Mr. Roto's son. His middle name, Minister, is his mother's maiden name. As for his first name, "My mom was adamant that she wanted unique names and Field is tied quite nicely to the career that I have. I feel very fortunate."

In early 2024 Yates told the *Boston Globe*, "I've been in a fantasy football league since I was 14, and know how those leagues connect people. I could talk about fantasy football 365 days a year."

A native of Weston, Mass., Yates attended Wesleyan University, where he earned a BA in psychology. He spent his summers as a ball boy for the New England Patriots, a job that he sums up as being "a human traffic cone in drills." He says he always wanted to work in football, either as a coach or a scout. "I think the players probably thought I was this little runt running around the facility, but the experience was priceless," he said. "That was my Rosetta Stone for football knowledge."

After graduation he got hired as an "operations intern" at the Kansas City Chiefs training camp in Wisconsin and hung on with the Chiefs, earning $22,000 his first year.

Landing a job with ESPN in 2012, he wrote for ESPN Boston and co-hosted a pair of ESPN Radio shows — "Operation Football" and "Football Friendzy." These days his main task at ESPN is hosting the Sunday morning series, "Fantasy Football Now," but he worries about spreading himself too thin. "Am I giving enough to everything? If I'm hosting 'NFL Live' does that mean I have to be more intentional with my fantasy football prep?

"Going into the season there are a lot of things that basically any reasonable fantasy analyst agrees on. So, what's tricky is that, it's not that my takes that I might have on my show are decidedly different from the takes that anybody else with a fantasy football opinion has, it's just that you try to deliver it in a more entertaining fashion.

"I hope that when people listen to our show, you want solid fantasy football advice, but you want to feel that for an hour or so it's like a suspension of reality for a little bit where you get to take your mind off of stuff and you hear things that you either agree or disagree upon."

Reflecting on the realities that come with his territory, Yates says, "I have a lot of 17-week friends. I only hear from them during the 17 weeks of the fantasy football season."

♦ ♦ ♦

Some people just enjoy ranking, and Jake Ciely of *The Athletic* (and the "All In Fantasy" podcast) is among them. For instance, ask him to name his favorite candy bar.

"Reese's. But only the holiday shapes because the texture is better."

Airline?

"None! But if I had to pick, Delta."

Sports-themed movie?

"Nobody would say this, but it's 'Rookie of the Year.'"

Breakfast cereal?

"Cinnamon Toast Crunch Churros. It doesn't get soggy the way regular Cinnamon Toast Crunch does."

When Ciely was hired in 2018, his bosses at *The Athletic* encouraged him to rank all sorts of things to emphasize the fact

Jake Ciely of The Athletic is willing to rank just about anything.

that he's one of fantasy football's most accurate rankers. Though data about the accuracy of top touts is not precise (more about which, below) Ciely has an enviable record.

Born in Passaic, New Jersey, Ciely's family moved to Virginia when he was eight. Armed with a degree in marketing from Old Dominion University, he took a job with the local Boar's Head meat distributor near his home in Virginia Beach. While at work one day in 2008 he received a call from a man who announced bluntly, "This is Tony Kornheiser."

"I felt the redness running up my back," Ciely recalls, as the caller asked, "So, what do you want?"

A bit of context: Ciely had been posting his thoughts about fantasy sports on Blogspot and had the audacity to mail a package of samples to 30 of the top sportswriters in America. Only two answered, the first being Kornheiser, the Emmy-winning ESPN host ("Pardon the Interruption") and acclaimed newspaper journalist. Ciely wasn't ready for such an important caller and was too nervous to ask proper questions. The call ended with Kornheiser essentially telling him to keep trying.

The second call, from ESPN's Mike Greenberg ("Sportscenter" and "Mike & Mike"), yielded the advice that Ciely should be contacting people who do the hiring, not the talent they've already hired. "It was the nicest 10 minutes I could imagine," says Ciely. "I wasn't ready for Tony, but maybe he got me ready for Mike."

Several years went by before Ciely landed a non-paying gig at RotoExperts.com covering basketball. Meanwhile, he and his father pursued another dream: They opened the All-In Gourmet Deli in Virginia Beach. Its highest ranking sandwich:

"The Pub. It was on toasted jalapeno cornbread. Sliced buffalo chicken with pepper jack cheese and this creamy horseradish sauce, plus lettuce, tomato and red onion. That thing sold like gangbusters."

After six months, Ciely's dad stepped away due to medical issues, leaving Jake working seven days a week while still writing for RotoExperts and becoming what his roommate described as "a miserable human being."

He declared bankruptcy in 2015.

RotoExperts helped him out with a paying job and a few years later *The Athletic* approached, as did NFL Network. Stumped about whether to make a move, Ciely reached out to Matthew Berry. "Take *The Athletic* job," said Berry. "It might not be the most money, but you're gonna go in like me, for them. You'll be the guy. Just listen to me, I know what I'm talking about."

When he started at *The Athletic*, Ciely was in as many as 30 seasonal redraft fantasy football leagues. "I've since cut back to just a handful, but I'm still doing a lot of best balls. Not much DFS. It feels like it's weighted to people who are really good at it. DFS has become all math and algorithms."

But he'll never give up ranking random stuff. "I'm just very opinionated is what it comes down to. I like opinions. I like debating. I like to, you know, argue a lot."

◆ ◆ ◆

With hundreds of "experts" offering fantasy football advice and rankings each week, it becomes a contest in itself to determine whom to trust.

FantasyPros has been charting the accuracy of prognosticators since 2009, when it determined that Yahoo's Andy Behrens was the season's most accurate NFL ranker. He edged out Pat Fitzmaurice of FantasyPros and Brandon Funston of Yahoo, with all three scoring just over 60 percent accuracy for 16 weeks.

"I'm glad someone runs an accuracy competition," Behrens told me, "because it gives analysts who are trying to build their brands a place to compete against those of us who work for mainstream media companies." But he adds this caveat: "Being an accurate ranker, by their definition or anyone's, doesn't mean someone is a good fantasy manager. It's a small piece of the content pie — although it definitely clicks well. Rankings are only as useful as the stories they tell. I think it's really admirable when someone takes an extreme outlier stance on a player in their ranks, but that's a pretty terrible way to work if you want to perform well in an accuracy contest."

Andrew Sears, President of FantasyPros, explains that he and the two co-founders, David Kim and Tom Nguyen, were fantasy football players, frustrated by the lack of info. "We would go to maybe like 10 different websites to get fantasy advice," he told me. "We saw an opportunity to aggregate the advice into one spot where you can get almost like the wisdom of the crowds. There was also the idea to measure accuracy of analysts, because nobody was doing that at the time. Fantasy football players didn't know who was giving the best advice. There wasn't any layer of accountability for the fantasy analysts."

Today, FantasyPros determines not only the accuracy of leading experts, it also provides the Expert Consensus Rankings (ECR) used by almost every site that provides fantasy football information. "We created a platform, an online ranker, where fantasy experts can create their rankings and have access to them 24/7. It's easy to manage updates and they can do it across different scoring formats. It became almost like a service to the fantasy experts where it made their lives easier. For us, it was an easy way to contribute to the accuracy competition as well. And the rankings that are submitted are part of the expert consensus, as well."

Beginning with the 2016 season, FantasyPros changed its methodology for determining the ranking of rankers. According to Sears, "We (now) look at the rankings on a per position basis. We use historical fantasy production to interpret those expert rankings as fantasy point projections, based off where the experts have ranked players. And then we compare those projections to how the players actually performed. We determine the difference ('gap'), and then we aggregate the scores across the entire season. Our mapping of point production for the rank spots uses the same historical production for both the expert's predicted ranks and the actual ranks. So, any expert who hits it on the head at predicting exactly the correct rank for a player will always get a zero error for that player."

Some analysts are displeased with the new system, and a few don't participate at all. Jake Ciely doesn't submit his ranking, noting that *The Athletic* prohibits its writers from taking part. Matthew Berry made his own decision to boycott FantasyPros, and I asked why. "I have a real issue on a personal level with how FantasyPros conducts its business. My personal opinion is that they are unethical. And it's not a company that I want to support in any way, shape or form."

Says Sears: "We take pride in having built a platform that showcases experts and provides tools to help them create their fantasy advice. Our track record of working with thousands of experts is a testament to the positive relationships we've developed in the fantasy industry. It's worth noting that Matthew Berry proudly displays our accuracy awards on his own website despite not wanting an association with FantasyPros."

Has FantasyPros ever booted out an "expert" for cheating by using someone else's rankings?

"Yes, we have. It's rare. But there have been one or two instances where we've had to take that step."

Among the honest brokers, who's the GOAT?

"I think if you look at it objectively," says Sears, "the person who has performed the best in our competitions has been Sean Koerner of the Action Network. He's finished in the top 10 in eight out of the 11 years that he's participated. He's won it four times. He's high on the list of someone who is trustworthy, because he's proven it time and time again."

Koerner runs the predictive analytics at Action Network and creates fantasy and betting content for the NFL, while also co-hosting the "Fantasy Flex" podcast as well as the betting show "Convince Me." He won the FantasyPros in-season ranking title in 2015, 2016 and 2017. In 2023 he came in first at ranking running backs, wide receivers and kickers; sixth with quarterbacks, ninth with tight ends and third with DST (defense and special teams). In second place was Elisha Twerski of *USA Today*; third went to Joe Bond of Fantasy Six Pack.

Koerner has been fascinated with sports betting and fantasy football ever since age 8, when his father took him to Las Vegas for his annual fantasy football draft. He began his betting career while getting a degree in psychology at Long Beach State — building sports betting models and becoming a bookie in college before moving to Vegas to work at Excalibur Sportsbook as a supervisor. Prior to joining Action in 2018, he worked for MGM, RotoHog and Bloomberg Sports.

♦ ♦ ♦

For every superstar fantasy pundit there are dozens, maybe hundreds, who work hard but struggle for attention. For instance, there's Cejaay Landry, a highly knowledgeable and super friendly guy who started playing fantasy football in the early '80s in British Columbia, in a league that mixed players from the NFL and the CFL. "The inherent problem," he recalls, "was that the Canadian Football League championship is in November, and the NFL was in January. So there was a month or so where you were getting rid of your players to try and pick up other players and it turned into a mess. So we just decided the next year just to do solely the NFL."

Landry has worked as a sportscaster on radio, served as a paid advisor to some top fantasy whales, and hosted a YouTube channel called "Dirty Landry's NFL Fantasy Report." As of this writing the channel has 72 videos and 95 subscribers — clearly not a big moneymaker, but a kind of warm and fuzzy take on the game. My favorite bit of advice from Cejaay is that fantasy managers ought to use a pencil and paper. "You look at your phone, with a little screen, and how do you know what you really have? You don't. So every week I write it out. Sometimes you forget who's on your bench. That's the old school way of doing it. By writing down all the stuff you retain it better."

Then there's the chiropractor and fantasy football fanatic Dr. Kevin Murray. In 2016 he was named "Commissioner of the Year" in a contest sponsored by ESPN and Pizza Hut. His local redraft league in Seattle, The Murray Fantasy League (MFL), was cited and the win earned Murray a diamond encrusted ring and a trip to ESPN's headquarters in Bristol, Connecticut. "I saw how you could stay connected with people that have been impactful throughout your whole life," he told me. "It's where I developed my passion for fantasy football."

That passion grew to include a website, Fantasy Football

Kevin Murray, wearing his diamond ring, with Field Yates at ESPN in Bristol.

Unlimited, and a podcast by the same name. "I really found my place in this industry as someone who supports others and promotes other people's works because I want people to fall deeper in love with the game." To that end, Murray has interviewed over 100 fantasy football analysts and writers, and archived them on his YouTube channel. The material doesn't get a lot of traffic, but it's a treasure trove for anyone curious about the people who make the industry tick. "The most common theme is passion for the game. It's so exciting to hear their stories and see how they've created opportunities for themselves."

Murray notes that the business of opining about fantasy football has become crowded. "There's not as much opportunity for monetary gain. So, most of these people have to be fueled by just enjoying it as a hobby. The passion for the hobby allows them to create content and have fun with it, and then potentially get picked up by bigger brands in order to find opportunity."

As fantasy football's content playing field becomes more crowded, everyone's seeking a media edge. "The dirty little secret is people want to be entertained more than they want really good information," notes Peter Overzet. "Maybe that was different early on. You know, when Matthew started, there were so few information sources. But these days, information is at anyone's fingertips. And so what makes people stand out is how entertaining are they. How is the packaging? Do they make it digestible? Is it fun? Is it not dry? And I think I've tried to come at it, similar to Matthew, from a fan approach of like, what is the kind of content I'd like to consume? I'm not the best analyst by any means. The guys out there with math brains and statistical brains run circles around me in that regard, but I think I can do a good job of taking those concepts and making them maybe more fun and interesting than they are on the surface."

Early on he attempted to combine his love for fantasy football with improv comedy. "We were doing some fantasy football comedy shows in a black box theater in Cambridge, Massachusetts for like 14 people and doing jokes that only we thought were funny."

But eventually Overzet developed some truly hilarious takes that mock the very craft — fantasy football analysis — that he specializes in. One of his characters is *Vinnie the Film Grinder* (with Jersey tough guy voice): "You guys look at your spreadsheets all day. Who's watching the tape? ... Tell me right now, can you see the hip swivel when you're looking at a spreadsheet? What Excel function has hip swivel!"

Then there's *Stan the Analytics Chaser* (with Woody Allen glasses and squeaky voice, commenting on the zero-RB strategy): "When we look at people who are drafting more than one running back in the first five rounds they're down to a 9.8 percent win rate. So you tell me, how are you going to sleep at night knowing your win rate has dropped 2.6 percentage points? ... You are mentally weak!"

Larry, the Obnoxious Co-worker (trying to get you to trade away Christian McCaffrey): "Come on dude, just look at your quarterback situation. Did I draft four quarterbacks that are useless on the market? Maybe. But you need a quarterback. ... What if McCaffrey breaks his leg?"

The Tweeter (who has reached 144 followers and is gushing with pride): "I know for a lot of you that might not mean much, but for me this is everything I've been building toward. I've been favoriting Matthew Berry's tweets for at least three years. ... I think I'm going to launch my own podcast. I'm just humbled to be here. And if I could just get into Scott Fish Bowl my entire life would be validated. Thank you guys so much for this journey. We're going to the moon!"

Comic and fantasy football guru Peter Overzet.

CHAPTER 9

The Players' Perspective

Jesus Loza with Austin Ekeler after making the playoffs in Ekeler's 2023 fantasy football competition.

The 2015 season involved bitter setbacks for Dallas quarterback Tony Romo — in both reality and fantasy. The Cowboys season began on a high note as Romo engineered a thrilling 27-26 win over the Giants, hitting tight end Jason Witten for a touchdown with seven seconds remaining. The following week Romo started hot against the Eagles but a sack in the third quarter broke his left collarbone and he was sidelined for eight weeks. Dallas lost every game during that stretch but managed a win in Romo's first game back. However, the following week, on Thanksgiving, he reinjured his shoulder against the Panthers, and Romo's season was done.

That same year Romo and two business partners organized what they called the National Fantasy Football Convention to be held at the Sands Expo Center in Las Vegas, an event that was to bring fans together with nearly 100 current and former players. Less than five weeks before the July date, an attorney for the league sent word that NFL players would be fined or suspended if they attended, because the event was being held at a casino property. In actuality, Romo's planned soiree was not technically in a casino, though it was near the Venetian hotel and casino. The event was canceled, and Romo's group sued the NFL for damages (the suit was later tossed out).

Despite the setback, Romo tried again the following year, this time at California's Pasadena Convention Center. The plan was to get far away from sportsbooks and take advantage of the big Los Angeles market, where fans were anticipating the return of the Rams from St. Louis. EA Sports and its popular Madden NFL video game were set to be a major sponsor, with fans playing the video game against NFL players in attendance. Conference marketing materials used the Madden logo — an image that includes the NFL's shield. NFL attorneys objected and EA Sports pulled out, forcing yet another cancellation.

Finally, in 2017, the event happened over a three-day weekend in Dallas. "I think the fans were blown away, I think the players were blown away," gushed Romo's partner Andy Alberth. "Everyone walked away with a memory, or a signature, or an autograph, maybe a photo."

Romo, who retired from football in 2017 and joined CBS Sports, was one of the first high-profile players to publicly embrace fantasy football, recognizing the synergy it provides fans and players. As Romo was attempting to launch his event that first year in Vegas, *Bleacher Report* conducted a small poll of two dozen active NFL players. Ten of 24 said they played fantasy football.

Today, there's not a lot of hard data about the number of real-life players in private fantasy leagues but it is legal. Unlike sports gambling, fantasy football is specifically allowed by the NFL, as long as it's not for big money. By rule:

"NFL Personnel may not accept prizes valued over Two Hundred Fifty Dollars ($250) in any fantasy football game. This prohibition is intended to avoid any appearance of impropriety which may result from participation in fantasy football games by individuals perceived to have an unfair advantage due to their preferential access to information."

Some NFL players, however, were jittery about possible cross pollination between fantasy and straight gambling. By 2024 the NFL commissioner Roger Goodell estimated that the league had disciplined "13 players and 25 league and team staffers" for gambling violations. Players are suspended one year for betting on the league and two for betting on their team. The policies for players betting on non-NFL sports while at a team facility or on team-related travel have relaxed, with first-time offenders receiving a two-game suspension without pay, second-time offenders six games and third-time offenders a year at minimum. Any inside information or third-party betting will result in an indefinite suspension of at least one year. Any actual or attempted game fixing will result in banishment from the league. Goodell said he spends a lot of time "educating, making sure that all of our personnel are aware of our gambling policies in this case, or any other policy that can affect the integrity of our game. So, ultimately, that's our primary job."

♦ ♦ ♦

When the Jaguars beat the Steelers 20-10 in Week 8 of the 2023 season, Jacksonville's star running back Travis Etienne Jr. had a big day, scoring 24 PPR fantasy points. His team won on the field, but Etienne lost on the computer. He tweeted: "I played against myself in fantasy fb today." He punctuated his message with a teary-eyed emoji.

Travis Etienne of the Jaguars not only plays fantasy football, he sometimes has to root against himself.

Minutes later, Matthew Berry tweeted a reply: "I can't believe your league wouldn't let you draft you. Or trade you back to you. But welcome to all of our pain of having to play against you. Congrats on a huge real life win."

However, not all NFL players had the same easy-going view about the fantasy game. At the close of the 2023 season players on the struggling Giants spoke with Dan Duggan of *The Athletic*. "I don't give a damn about fantasy," wide receiver Sterling Shepard said. According to Duggan most of the Giants skill players expressed similar feelings but got frequent reminders about fantasy football through messages on social media about their performances. "I definitely get a lot of tweets and DMs and mentions," running back Saquon Barkley (now with the Eagles) said. "I think two weeks ago, I definitely didn't help anybody. I don't know how you score those points — I probably had like zero." Indeed, Barkley's fantasy owners were miffed when he had just 14 yards on nine carries, plus two catches for 23 yards, in the Giants' 24-6 loss to the Saints in Week 15.

"I remember when I tore my ACL (in 2020), people were talking about, 'You fucked up my fantasy team,'" Barkley said. "I was like, 'Bro, I'm worried about surgery. I really don't care about your fantasy team right now.'"

But tight end Darren Waller, who retired before the 2024 season, acknowledged the importance of fantasy to the league. "People are tuned in to every game," he said. "Somebody in Atlanta will be tuned into the Cardinals and the Seahawks because they've got Kyler Murray. It's great for the fans to stay engaged."

"I'm a competitor so I love the fact that people are trying to build a team and trying to beat their family members or their friends in a fantasy championship," Barkley said. "My goal is to go out there and compete at a high level and make plays for my team. If I can do that and that helps someone win a fantasy championship, then so be it."

Across the pro sports landscape there is growing concern about ways in which disgruntled fans and gamblers are taking out their frustrations. An alarming report by Bob Nightengale in *USA Today* looked at problems encountered in baseball. He wrote: "They receive death threats. They are followed home by strangers. They are abused and derided. They are Major League

Baseball players, who can tell you all about the menacing threats that have been inflicted upon their lives since MLB and gambling companies got into bed together."

I asked Marcas Grant, who has covered fantasy for more than a decade from inside NFL headquarters, how the players feel. "I think when you hear the pushback and frustration from players, it's more about the reactions that they get on social media. When you have a bad day at work you don't want 1,000 people telling you about it. When a player has a bad game they don't want to go on social media and get all these notifications of people basically screaming at them about how you cost me a fantasy matchup. But I do think there are a lot more players who do like it, who are involved with fantasy football and play it.

"I think you have a generation of athletes who, even if they don't play, they know all about it. When they get drafted they don't shy away from the question of why should people draft you on their fantasy team? Whereas once upon a time, I think guys were a little hesitant to answer that question. I think guys are a little more open about it now because fantasy football has been there for most of their lives."

◆ ◆ ◆

One NFL player who is all-in on fantasy football is running back Austin Ekeler, now with the Commanders, who is a hard-core fantasy player. He's also an investor in Matthew Berry's Fantasy Life company. His nonprofit, the Austin Ekeler Foundation, runs an annual fantasy football tournament using the Yahoo platform, with buy-ins between $500 and $5,000 and prizes including cash, rings and a dinner with Ekeler.

Austin Ekeler takes a handoff in practice from his new teammate Jayden Daniels.

In 2023 Ekeler also teamed with Yahoo to create a 14-team fantasy league for media professionals. Ekeler envisions it becoming a bigger event, saying, "I think we're on the verge of something so I'm super excited." With the #4 pick, Matt Harmon of Yahoo Sports drafted Ekeler. "I was like, 'Damnit,'" said Ekeler, "the only thing I wanted to get in this draft was myself." Ekeler wound up with the last draft slot at #14 and with his two picks at the turn he took receiver Davante Adams and running back Josh Jacobs.

Ekeler might be the NFL's top fantasy booster. "It's what gives depth to the viewership of the NFL," he says. "Sports betting and fantasy sports give so much more engagement for fan to be actually invested."

"Some players have really leaned into it," notes Yahoo's Andy Behrens. "Ekeler is a good example, but there are many others who predate Ekeler, who have a real understanding that this is very good for their personal brands and their profiles. You'll almost never hear Austin complain about people giving him crap on social media, if he has a poor game or if he declines to score a touchdown or something like that. He's very aware of keeping fantasy managers happy and addressing fantasy managers, because he just knows it's kind of good business. And he's interested in the game. You have other players who couldn't care less about it."

Rick Wolf says he understands when NFL players get angry if fantasy players cross the line. "The fantasy industry frowns on it," he told me, "and when they see it, they attack it quickly. Matthew Berry is one of the big watchdogs. He has such a huge following that if somebody attacks Austin Ekeler, he'll be the next one to post that the guy, you know, is not a real fantasy player because he's attacking the athletes who make our game so great."

CHAPTER 10
Celebrities Huddle Up

Diehards Will Ferrell and Ryan Reynolds at Super Bowl LVI.

Tens of thousands of fantasy football players have a league at the office, but only a dozen of them are part of The Office League.

Marking its 19th season in 2024, the league gets its name from the acclaimed TV series "The Office," where all 12 members worked during the show's nine seasons. (The league is listed on the Yahoo platform with its official name, "Dunder Mifflin.") Among the fantasy players: Brian Baumgartner (Kevin Malone), John Krasinski (Jim Halpert), Rainn Wilson (Dwight Schrute) and Andy Buckley (David Wallace). The other eight players were staff and crew, including the commissioner, Stephen Saux, who was a stand-in and also delivered a line or two in occasional bit parts. "When we began this," Saux recalls, "there was no online draft. We started doing the draft on a yellow legal pad and it would take us weeks. There was no time limit. When it was your turn to draft you got handed the yellow legal pad. Then you would have to make your pick but you might be in the middle of a scene and it could take hours or it could be passed to me and I could have gone home for the day."

Saux says he took the commissioner job because no one else wanted it. "I love fantasy football," he says. "Besides corralling everybody and dispensing a little bit of money, I'm able to be

THE Hollywood REPORTER

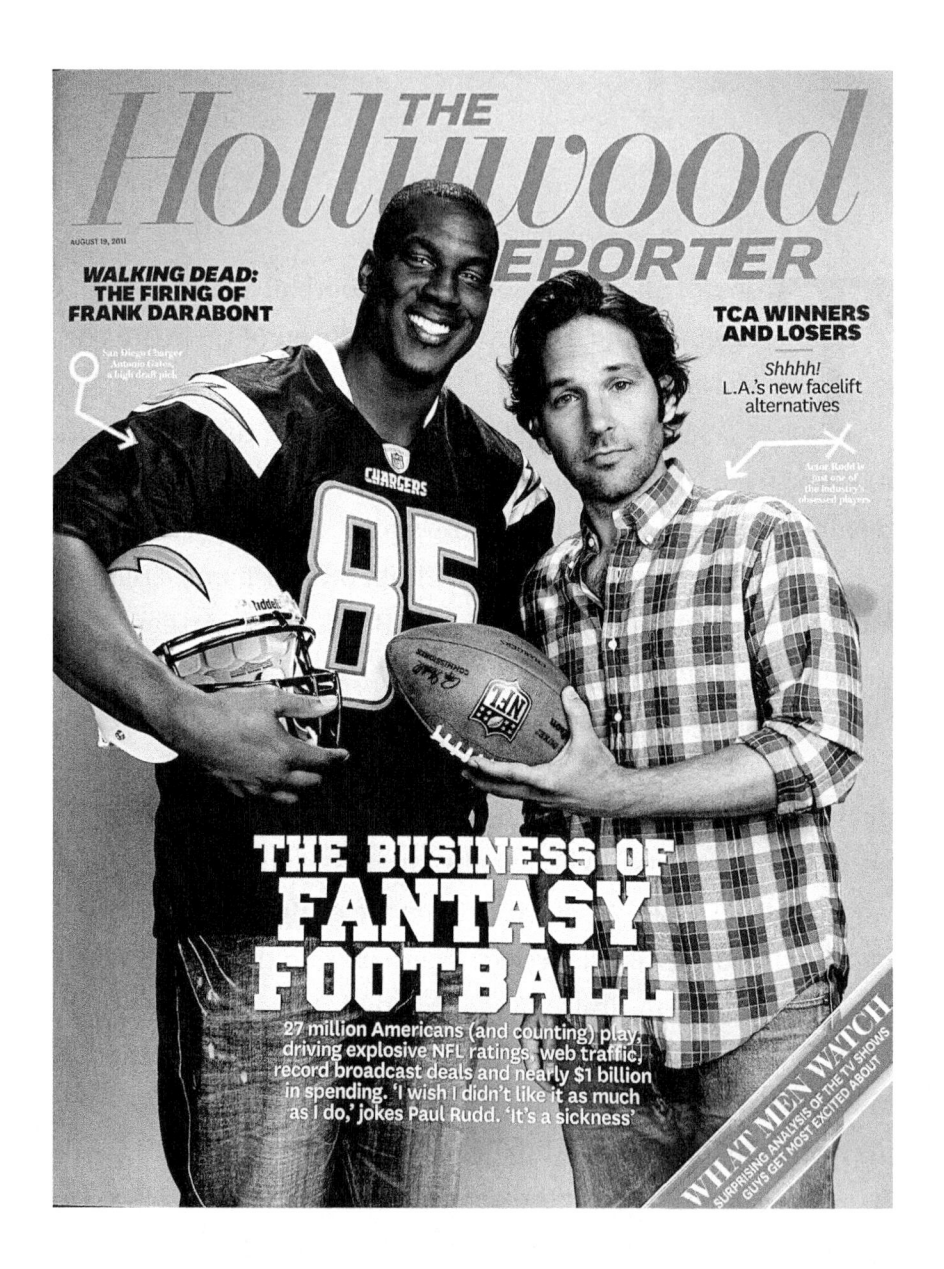

AUGUST 19, 2011

WALKING DEAD: THE FIRING OF FRANK DARABONT

San Diego Charger Antonio Gates, a high draft pick

TCA WINNERS AND LOSERS

Shhhh! L.A.'s new facelift alternatives

Actor Rudd is just one of the industry's obsessed players

THE BUSINESS OF FANTASY FOOTBALL

27 million Americans (and counting) play, driving explosive NFL ratings, web traffic, record broadcast deals and nearly $1 billion in spending. 'I wish I didn't like it as much as I do,' jokes Paul Rudd. 'It's a sickness'

WHAT MEN WATCH SURPRISING ANALYSIS OF THE TV SHOWS GUYS GET MOST EXCITED ABOUT a facilitator of us staying together. It really is fantastic because there's a lot of ribbing that goes on between us. We're close like family."

"It's pretty cutthroat," says Wilson, who has one win to his credit. "Rainn talks more trash than anyone," explains Baumgartner. "Week to week, when you are competing against him, you will hear from him almost daily — and on Sundays, multiple times, giving you updates on how much he's kicking your ass, even though you're looking at it at the same time."

Across show business there have been numerous fantasy football leagues. One of the most publicized was the AGBO Superhero Fantasy Football Charity League, featuring big-name stars playing for charity. With a $1,250,000 donation from FanDuel in 2020, a million dollars was awarded to the charities selected by participants, based in part on their standings. The league was founded by "Avengers: Endgame" director Joe Russo, celebrity fantasy football league commissioner Guillermo Lozano, and NBC fantasy football expert Matthew Berry. The 14-team league included Chris Evans, Paul Rudd, Chris Pratt, Robert Downey Jr., Tom Holland, Ryan Reynolds and Elizabeth Olsen.

Berry is reluctant to talk about who might have needed some help with draft picks. "You don't usually draft quarterbacks first," he notes, "so I was surprised Rudd took Mahomes as his number one pick. But he's a huge Kansas City guy so it kind of makes sense." Rudd is such a big Fantasy Football fan that his wife often gets mad at him for playing. "I wish I didn't like it as much as I do," he says. "It's a sickness."

Berry helped Jay-Z draft his team, and says the rapper is

Jay-Z, Matthew Berry, Chris Paul.

"one of the greatest trash talkers in the history of fantasy football." He plays in a 12-team three-wide receiver, half-point per reception league. According to Berry, Jay-Z's inside knowledge is almost unfair because he knows most of the top NFL players personally.

♦ ♦ ♦

A diehard fantasy football player, NBC latenight host Seth Meyers still meets up with his old friends every year for an in-person draft. It's a 12-team standard scoring league where there's a limit on the number of players per position; you can only have four running backs at any one time. The annual prize in Meyers' league is not having to travel. Each year everyone goes to the winner's home for the draft — which in 2023 was in Minnesota.

Meyers' colleague at NBC, Jimmy Fallon, wrote one of his "thank-you notes" about his beloved fantasy football game:

Seth Meyers, singer Brett Kissel, take the field.

"Thank you, fantasy football draft, for letting me know that even in my fantasies I am bad at sports."

♦ ♦ ♦

Actor Jeff Garlin, who viewers know best as Jeff Greene on "Curb Your Enthusiasm," is a Bears season ticket-holder in his native Chicago and a hardcore fantasy football player. Asked by *The Athletic* about "expert" advice to fantasy managers, he minced no words. "I gotta truly tell you people don't know what the fuck they're talking about. I do fantasy football and I read the experts. I don't know where the word expert comes in. I truly could be an expert tomorrow. I know as much as these guys if I put the effort in. That being said, they know football and stuff. But nobody knows anything. Really."

♦ ♦ ♦

Professional athletes in other sports are among the most dedicated fantasy football fans. "Pretty much every Major League

Baseball clubhouse has an active fantasy football league," notes Yahoo's Andy Behrens. According to *The New York Times*, "There may not be a group of individuals more devoted to fantasy football than baseball players."

A league run by Angels superstar Mike Trout made headlines in 2022 when Reds outfielder Tommy Pham slapped the Giants' Joc Pederson during batting practice on May 29 — all because of a GIF sent to the fantasy football league's group chat. Pham was suspended for three games and called Trout "the worst commissioner in fantasy sports."

Trout, an obsessive Eagles fan, said there's a waiting list for his league — which has a $10,000 buy-in for participants.

♦ ♦ ♦

Actor and comedian Will Ferrell plays in what he calls a "mega-fantasy expert league" with 360 people. "The conferences are named after Will Ferrell things," he says, "like 'Anchorman,' 'Zoolander,' 'Step Brothers,' etc. Then each conference has five different 12-team divisions in it, with names like, 'Dorothy Mantooth Division,' 'I Love Lamp Division' and 'Sex Panther Division.' All the team names are just our real names, though."

Ferrell played some football in school, where he says his favorite move as a defensive back was to size up the runner for the tackle and then, at the last minute, grab his face mask. After one season he was demoted to kicker.

♦ ♦ ♦

Comic David Spade extended his love for fantasy football to accepting a role on Fox Sports 1's "Fantasy Football Uncensored." Hosted by analyst Jay Glazer, the series lasted only

David Spade is joined by NFL cheerleaders to pitch "Fantasy Football Uncensored."

through the 2014 season. Spade's pitch to viewers: "Hey guys! What are you doing for the next 17 weeks? Why don't you watch eight idiots battle it out in fantasy football? We'll give you everything: stats, injury reports, and projected court appearances of all the players!"

Appearing with Spade was Nick Swardson, a Minnesota native who remains a diehard Vikings fan, known for playing Terry Bernadino in the comedy series "Reno 911!" Swardson posted on Facebook:

"Dear guy who started fantasy football, thanks for making me sad and suicidal on Mondays. Making hangovers a thousand times worse. (Or maybe I shouldn't have drafted a shit team.)"

♦ ♦ ♦

Jon Hamm, the acclaimed actor perhaps best known for his role as Don Draper in "Mad Men," has a long history of frustrations in fantasy football. A low point came in 2014 when Bill Simmons — who was still writing for ESPN at the time — kicked him out of a "survivor" league. "There's no rhyme or reason to it," Hamm said. "Whoever wins the league picks. They pick the person who's out, and you don't know until draft day."

♦ ♦ ♦

Actor Jerry Ferrara, best known for his role as Turtle on the HBO comedy series "Entourage," is big on fantasy football. He had an online show based on his fantasy football league, "The Gentlemen's League." Back in 2011 Ferrara wrote an article about his obsession:

"Some of you might not get people's infatuation with fantasy football. In fact, there have been times I've wondered myself. ... When people ask, 'Why the obsession with fantasy?' I usually just launch into the details of how to play. They look at me like I'm nuts. I realize now, that's the wrong answer: The real answer is as corny as a man telling a woman, 'You complete me.'

"It's friendship. That is the obsession. I've been in the same fantasy league for six years, made up of some of my closest friends, including a few who weren't friends until fantasy football. I know this is way cornier than I expected; I even deleted this whole thing a few times. But it's true. Fantasy football is my guarantee that I will be in constant contact with my friends.

"Whether it's draft night, phone calls of trades offers or simply watching 'Monday Night Football' with our game hanging

FANTASY LEAGUE KICK OUT REVEALED!

After being kicked out of his league for a year, Jon Hamm joined the draft via Zoom to eliminate another member.

in the balance, it all adds up to my friendship security blanket. I know it shouldn't take a Dungeons & Dragons-type game to bring friends together. Most of the time, it doesn't. But let's be honest: Sometimes life just gets in the way of friendship. Fantasy football gives us a carved out, set-in-cement friendship routine."

♦ ♦ ♦

Many celebrities and sports writers, plus a growing number of average Joes, participate in a fantasy football event named after the guy who started it in 2010, Scott Fish. Appropriately, he named it The Scott Fish Bowl.

A few years later Fish expanded his project to include a non-profit called Fantasy Cares, which uses entry fees from the fantasy football competition for charitable donations, starting with Toys for Tots. Launched with 96 players, the Scott Fish Bowl has grown to involve thousands of players worldwide and

A large, enthusiastic crowd turned out for the Scott Fish Bowl draft in Los Angeles.

has raised hundreds of thousands for charity, with drafts conducted in numerous locations in early July.

A breakthrough came in 2023 when Underdog agreed to run a satellite tournament for Fantasy Cares. Fifteen thousand participants pay $5 on the Underdog site to enter a best ball contest, with the entire pot of $75,000 going to charity. There are no cash prizes for players, but the top 500 finishers get a spot in the main Scott Fish Bowl event.

When he was honored with Matthew Berry's "Game Changer" award in 2021, Fish said, "It is amazing the way this industry supports and recognizes charitable efforts. I love that adding purpose to the games we love and play has become increasingly integrated into the industry. It helps both grow and connect our community."

Fish hopes that every fantasy football league makes at least a small donation to charity. "Imagine 100,000 leagues giving 10 bucks each. That's a million dollars — and you know we can go way over that. Do some good with this hobby of ours."

His motto: "Work hard. Be a good person. Everything else will follow."

CHAPTER 11

The Richest 2 Percent

Michael Cohen, a hedge fund trader from Texas, has won multiple millions in fantasy football.

The University of Connecticut catalog provides these details about David Bergman, an associate professor who teaches operations and information management in the School of Business:

"Areas of Expertise and Interest — Large-scale automated decision making, decision diagrams, discrete optimization, integer programming, machine learning, integration of optimization techniques." Translation: This guy could be really good at fantasy football.

Indeed, in 2021 the UConn website carried this headline:

Business Professor Wins $2.5 Million Fantasy Football Jackpot Using the Concepts He Teaches Students

For Bergman (whose handle is "theWhistlesGoWhooo") the only downside to winning the DraftKings Fantasy Football World Championship was that his pals kicked him out of the seasonal league he'd been a part of since his undergraduate days at Stony Brook University. He had become just too good. According to my back-of-envelope computation, Bergman has won over $20 million playing DFS contests, primarily fantasy football.

"It's something I do every single day in nearly every single sport," he said when I asked about his DFS diet. "I mean, it's what

I do. I came in second place one year in the golf world championships, came in fourth place in the basketball world championships and I've won Milly Makers outside of that big win."

But football is Bergman's passion. To win the $2.5 million he constructed a lineup featuring Arizona's Kyler Murray at QB, stacked with WR DeAndre Hopkins and RB Chase Edmonds. Murray smashed with 406 yards passing and three TDs, plus 29 yards on the ground and another TD. Hopkins caught nine passes for 169 yards and a TD, while Edmonds added 66 total yards and a TD. (Edmonds was owned by just 1% in the DraftKings competition.) "I entered this with the intention of having fun," he said that day, "and I'm still in it to have fun — I'm just a few million dollars richer."

The university was quick to cash-in on its own bet. Immediately after Bergman's big DraftKings haul, Jose Cruz, associate dean of graduate programs in the School of Business, cited it as an example of how students obtain "real-world experience," and boasted that, "David's winning is just an example of what (the UConn) curriculum prepares students to do."

That might be a bit hyperbolic, since there is no evidence that any of Bergman's students has succeeded in DFS at anything approaching their teacher's level. Yet, Bergman explains, "My final project for some of my classes is to play against me in a daily fantasy sports competition, of course, for free. "I typically don't win those, which means that my students are actually learning quite a bit."

Indeed, his students are enthusiastic. "He used the analytics to actually win a huge bet, and that was the most impressive thing that I've ever heard in my entire life," Siddherdh

David Bergman at UConn in 2021.

Rajguru, an MBA candidate told WVIT-TV in Connecticut at the time of Bergman's big win. Another student, Ankit Lohia, added, "It feels amazing, like how you can play with numbers and make business decisions, and in terms of sports betting as well because it's a great opportunity. … If a student is good enough with his statistics skills and his predictive skills, why can't he pursue a career in sports betting?"

As Bergman sees it, "There is a wide range of DFS players. Some are more intuitive, some are more analytical players, and there are people who fall within that spectrum. I am definitely more of an analytics person — almost all of it done with AI, machine learning and optimization." Most of the software is proprietary, built by Bergman himself.

I asked him about his secret sauce. "I don't have any standard, single model," he said. "I change my models every day. I go for more wild picks some days, more conservative picks the other days. It also depends on how the field is moving. It's really hard to pin down what I do because I don't do anything consistently."

Except win.

♦ ♦ ♦

A frequently cited statistic in DFS football is that less than 2 percent of the players win roughly 98 percent of the money. But that hasn't dampened the popularity of big tournaments, which have grown since 2013 when an Iowa sales manager named Travis Spieth invested $10 in FanDuel's Fantasy Football Championship and became daily fantasy's first one-day million-dollar winner. As mentioned earlier, a personal trainer from California, Scott Hanson, was soon crowned the first daily fantasy multimillionaire by winning the $2 million grand prize.

♦ ♦ ♦

On Two Gun Way in the Houston suburb of Katy, one of fantasy football's biggest winners not only makes his home — he owns the street.

Michael Cohen (not the Trump lawyer), whose handle on DraftKings and FanDuel is "twogun," is a multiple million-dollar winner. Naturally, when he used some of his prize money to buy houses and land on Dewberry Street, one of the first things he did was get the name legally changed to Two Gun Way.

Like many skilled DFS players, Cohen found his way to fantasy football through poker, working on what he calls a "poker strategy website" while studying at Northwestern. Taking a job as a hedge fund trader — a profession he's still engaged in today — Cohen's friends introduced him to fantasy football through a site called DraftDay, which, between 2011 and 2014 claimed to have paid out over $40 million in winnings. Cohen got his first taste of big profits in 2013 on another site, Fan Throwdown, where he won $100,000. In Week 17 the following year he had multiple winners in a DraftKings contest, including first place, for a payday of $700,000. His best selection was low-owned Eric Decker, the Jets wide receiver, who wound up with 10 catches for 221 yards and a TD, making him the NFL's top WR for the week. "I ended up naming my son after him," Cohen told me. "His name is Ezra Decker Cohen."

Michael Cohen, on the street he bought with his winnings, honoring his handle "twogun."

Two weeks after his Week 17 win, Cohen won his first million-dollar prize on DraftKings. As of this writing, he has won the Milly Maker's top prize five different times.

The handle twogun goes back to a title Cohen saw in a used book shop, "Morris Two-Gun Cohen," which tells the true story of a Canadian con artist who went to China and became an arms dealer. Once grazed by a bullet, he took to carrying two guns for protection. "When I started playing online poker they asked for my handle, so I just said, 'Two Gun.'"

Though Cohen uses computer stats to make his lineups, he tends to rely on his own analysis and instinct more than most other successful DFS players. "I'm looking at the same generic things that everyone else sees — like who's injured, who's starting — stuff you can get from Twitter. When it comes to subjective information, that's where I limit caring about what other people say. I do care about ownership projections.

"There are some players who are very algorithmic. It's just not my style — in DFS or in the stock market. I think I'm pretty good at understanding how you can have an edge against large groups and group-think. Football is a high variance game, so sometimes people trust the algorithms a little too much. At the end of the day, one big play can be the difference in the week. It's respecting that and respecting the variances in football that makes me a good player."

♦ ♦ ♦

On a slow week, the DFS whale Youda Cao spends $500,000 in entry fees. During busy weeks — which for him means during all or most of the NFL season — he puts over a million dollars on the line. He's won many millions and has been ranked at various times by RotoGrinders as the nation's number one DFS player. He's also lost a lot, which during his worst "downswings" has reached "two or three million." At the bottom line: His ROI (return on investment) in high stakes DFS is a bit over 5 percent — giving him an average annual profit of nearly $3 million.

"Youdacao," as he's known on DraftKings ("booourns" on FanDuel), doesn't do much conventional sports wagering, mainly because he sees his primary skill as outsmarting a field of other entrants, not beating the House. Moreover, high stakes DFS players don't have to worry about being "limited" by sportsbooks, which is what happens to gamblers who win too much in straight betting. The reason is simple: In DFS entry fees go into a pot from which the operator takes a fee (usually between 9 and 11 percent), and the balance is paid out in prizes. There is no risk for the operator. In straight gambling, however, the sportsbook is on the hook to cover its losses (although major sportsbooks are skilled at avoiding that, in large part by limiting big winners).

In Underdog's Best Ball Mania V, for example, 672,672 entrants paid $25 each to create a pot of $16,816,800. Underdog's "rake," or "service fee," was 10.8 percent, giving the company a gross profit of $1,816,214 on that contest. The remaining $15,000,586 was paid out in prizes. In that type of business model there is no reason to place limits, except to cap the number of entries from any single account, usually at 150.

Youda Cao started playing fantasy sports for no money as a small child. He went on to develop skills in finance, economics and technology, providing a foundation for his DFS play, which he began pursuing seriously in 2015. For many years he was a big winner, while remaining silent, even somewhat mysterious, about himself and his process. After winning yet another Milly Maker on DraftKings in NFL Week 9 in 2023, he opened up in interviews with Peter Overzet and Adam Levitan, but declined my requests to be interviewed for this book.

"My setup is in a dingy guest room in my house," he said. "I've got two laptops with two separate mouses — you have more control, you're not going to randomly be on the wrong screen. ... I watch the games. I think it's valuable for picking up things that will help in your future decision making. ... My projections have always been my own.

"For the NFL I won't even touch anything until Friday morning and I don't start making projections until Saturday. Sunday I'm up at 6 a.m. building, because that's how long it takes to pump out 150 lineups.

"My process is super no-frills. It might as well be just: Work hard."

Looking back at his 10-year career as a DFS pro, "I don't think it's gotten that much harder, it's just more analytically inclined now. The industry has gotten better at stacking and projecting. For a new player coming in, it's never been tougher."

Youda Cao has one piece of wisdom that fantasy football players at all levels can appreciate. "There's rarely a really bad play," he says, "because if you create a really shitty lineup you can just say it's contrarian."

♦ ♦ ♦

Underdog's "Best Ball Mania" has produced several millionaire winners, but none involves a story with more drama — and "sweat" as the fantasy world calls it — than Pat Kerrane's experience on January 2, 2023 when he won the $2 million first prize — though for three torturous days it was in doubt.

It came down to the Bills-Bengals game on Monday night, with Kerrane holding a slim lead among 470 finalists in BBM3 (the contest had 450,000 entries at the start of the season). Kerrane didn't have anyone in the game, so all he could do was hope his opponents wouldn't catch up. An early touchdown by Bengals receiver Tyler Boyd didn't help. The Bills followed with a field goal. Then, with about six minutes remaining in the opening quarter, the unthinkable happened.

"And now another Bills player is down," said Joe Buck on ESPN.

"I can't tell exactly who that is," remarked Troy Aikman.

"Maybe Hamlin," said Buck.

It took paramedics nine minutes to revive Damar Hamlin, who had fallen to the ground at 8:55 p.m. after making a routine tackle on receiver Tee Higgins. A ring of players knelt, some of them weeping. Kerrane was watching at his Brooklyn, N.Y. apartment, while also doing a live stream on YouTube's "Ship Chasing" channel. His buddy Peter Overzet and others on the show had been rooting for Kerrane to take down the big prize, but now, in a surreal moment, they shut down the stream and stared at the TV screen. Three days went by, with Kerrane afraid to tell his family that he had millions on the line, fearing he might still lose out if the game were resumed.

By Thursday Hamlin's condition and prognosis improved,

Pat Kerrane on "Legendary Upside."

and the NFL finally announced that the game would not be completed; all records were voided. Underdog declared Pat Kerrane the $2 million winner.

"I started playing fantasy football when I was 14," Kerrane explains. "The scoring settings were a disaster. We had something absurd like 0.5 points per carry, and I'm pretty sure there were 0 points per reception. I thought Eddie George, who averaged 3.7 yards per carry on 403 carries in the 2000 season, was the height of fantasy football excellence."

Kerrane grew up in Delaware and got a master's in energy policy at the University of Delaware, where both his parents worked. He moved to New York in 2011 for a job with an energy company, but was growing more "obsessed" with playing fantasy football and listening to Matthew Berry's podcast. He began writing for RotoViz (the site that broke through in 2013 by introducing the "Zero RB" draft strategy). At about that time he and his younger brother, Mike, created a site they called "Roto-

Blurb," which contained humorous fake notes about NFL players. Pat applied for a job with RotoWorld at NBC Sports, where he was asked, "Can you blurb?" because blurbing is a big part of service. "Well," he told them, "I did start a fake version of your site," and he was soon hired. "RotoWorld had an app that serious fantasy players would check every day," Kerrane told me. "That's how you would stay up to date on the news. And it did have a bit of humor to it."

For Kerrane, the "life changing" story began in 2022 — on July 18, to be precise — when he was scheduled to do a live best ball draft on a podcast. To prepare, he did a draft on Underdog, experimenting with strategies, such as rostering three quarterbacks. Drafting in the seventh position (among 12 participants) Kerrane took Chargers running back Austin Ekeler with his first pick. He added Giants RB Saquon Barkley second and Panthers receiver D.J. Moore third. He waited until the eighth round to take quarterback Tom Brady of the Bucs and later added the Dolphins Tua Tagovailoa and the Giants Daniel Jones.

After that day, as is often the case with best ball, Kerrane lost focus on the roster — one of 150 he drafted in BBM3. Not until Week 15 of the season, when Underdog trimmed the field, did he start paying attention. In Week 16, Ekeler scored two touchdowns, helping propel Kerrane to the 470-team final. In Week 17 Ekeler had 161 total yards and two TDs, for 30.1 fantasy points. D.J. Moore added 20.7 fantasy points and Tom Brady smashed with 37.7.

"This team was built for Week 17 to an almost comical degree," Kerrane recalls. "Pete (Overzet) had done a video that summer titled, 'Week 17 Is All That Matters,' that was really

> **Underdog Fantasy** @UnderdogFantasy · Follow
>
> Congratulations to @PatKerrane for taking home 1st Place and $2,000,000 in BBMIII
>
> Thank you to everyone who played NFL Best Ball with us this season

	PLAYER • POSITION	PICK	WK 17 POINTS
UNDERDOG FANTASY	AUSTIN EKELER - RB	1.10	30.1
	SAQUON BARKLEY - RB	2.03	6.3
BBMIII	DJ MOORE - WR	3.10	20.7
	JAYLEN WADDLE - WR	4.03	7.8
	GEORGE KITTLE - TE	5.10	10.3
FIRST PLACE	CHRIS GODWIN - WR	6.03	16.5
$2,000,000	HUNTER RENFROW - WR	7.10	3.4
TEAM DRAFTED ON JULY 18	TOM BRADY - QB	8.03	37.68
	TYLER LOCKETT - WR	9.10	2.5
	RHAMONDRE STEVENSON - RB	10.03	6.1
	JAKOBI MEYERS - WR	11.10	13.0
	TUA TAGOVAILOA - QB	12.03	0
	MIKE GESICKI - TE	13.10	6.8
	DANIEL JONES - QB	14.03	36.10
TOM BRADY 37.68	WAN'DALE ROBINSON - WR	15.10	0
AUSTIN EKELER 30.1	RAHEEM MOSTERT - RB	16.03	10.7
DJ MOORE 20.7	SONY MICHEL - RB	17.10	0
	TYQUAN THORNTON - WR	18.03	12.5

In its rush to post the results of BBM3, Underdog had Kerrane drafting 10th; in fact, he was 7th. "Fortunately, the prize money was not a typo," he said later.

influential." It noted that the Bucs faced the Panthers in Week 17, so Kerrane had Brady and Chris Godwin on the Bucs and was able to "bring it back" with D.J. Moore on the Panthers — in what turned out to be a high scoring game, with Tampa Bay winning 30-24.

With the prize money, Kerrane was able to give up his one-bedroom apartment in Brooklyn and move to San Diego where he launched his own site, Legendary Upside. For years he had been reluctant to make a full-time career move. "I decided, okay, I'm going to do something that I can grow myself and have a lot of fun."

Like Mason Dodd and numerous others who have crowded into the best ball space, Kerrane has an engaging on-camera presence that makes his analysis both informative and entertaining — without going over the top. And, like the others, he now has a partnership arrangement with Underdog through which customers get a site credit for signing up, while he gets a commission.

Austin Ekeler joined Kerrane in an NBC interview, saying, "I just want to thank you for supporting your boy and picking me. I'm glad we could get that W together. Enjoy those winnings and remember: I'm always a pretty good pick for you in the future as well."

◆ ◆ ◆

Al Zeidenfeld burst onto the DFS scene in 2012 and quickly established himself as a dominant player in several sports. Known on the poker circuit back then as "Al Smooth," he found that the handle wasn't available on DFS sites, so he switched to "Al_Smizzle." A year later he was cruising toward the million-dollar top prize in the 2013 DraftKings Fantasy Football Champi-

Al Zeidenfeld, aka Al Smizzle.

onship — until Frank Gore ruined it. With about five minutes remaining in the 49ers-Falcons game, Gore bulled his way up the middle for a one-yard TD, leaving Zeidenfeld trailing on DK by 0.8 points, good for second place and a meager $350,000 prize.

Before DFS Zeidenfeld had been a ninth-grade girls' basketball coach, but even at that level strategy was his game. "My big thing was always to mix people up," he told journalist Daniel Barbarisi. "It's the same thing in poker, the same thing in coaching. I can manipulate it. I know what they're going to do, and I use it against them."

His second-place win — and his larger-than-life personality — caught the attention of multiple media outlets who hired him as a fantasy commentator. DraftKings brought him onboard as a "brand ambassador." Then, two weeks into the 2016 season, while he was dishing out DFS advice on ESPN and co-hosting "The Edge" podcast presented by DraftKings, he invested $3,000 for 150 entries in the Milly Maker, which attracted a total of 277,286 lineups. With one lineup collecting 221.32 points, Zeidenfeld picked up the million-dollar first prize — along with some headaches.

The previous year a DraftKings employee named Ethan Haskell won $350,000 in a DFS competition — on FanDuel. He was accused of using confidential information about ownership trends to set his lineup. Though cleared of any legal wrongdoing, Haskell's experience brought DFS under closer scrutiny by state lawmakers. So, when Al Smizzle picked up his million, some eyebrows were raised. DraftKings issued a statement: "Al Zeidenfeld is an expert DFS player who is an independent contractor and brand ambassador; he shares his tips and expertise with the DFS player community. He is not a DraftKings employee, and does not have access to contest data or any other non-public company information."

He was once asked on "The Football Guys" podcast to speculate if he found himself on death row, what he would request for his last meal. Al Smizzle's answer reflected why he's so entertaining and quick-witted when opining about fantasy football. "Anything that you can hide a key in," he said.

CHAPTER 12
Leagues of Their Own

Samantha Holt and Kendall Valenzuela of Fantasy Life, with Underdog VP Stacie Stern (center).

"I was ready to throw in the towel on DFS football because I had done so poorly. I felt I was never going to win any money. I was frustrated."

That was Alisha Hunt's downbeat view the morning of Sunday, December 4, 2022. A life-long sports fan, living with her fiancé, Leslie, in the Chicago suburb of Arlington Heights, Hunt decided to limit herself to just three lineups in DraftKings Milly Maker tournament for Week 13 (as many as 150 lineups were allowed, at $20 a pop). She conjured up three and went back to sleep.

I've always liked to gamble and frequent the casinos," she told me. "I'm not really great at regular fantasy sports, where it's a season-long thing, but I feel I have a knack for DFS."

Like most participants in big tournaments, Hunt looks for contrarian players and stacks that might click on a given week. That morning she focused on Geno Smith, the Seahawks quarterback, who was only 1.87 percent owned, and his receiver Tyler Lockett, who was rostered at just 5.14 percent. Seattle was facing the Rams and "I believe the Rams defense was pretty bad at the time, so I thought the Smith-Lockett stack was a great pick."

Alisha Hunt sets her lineup.

Waking about 30 minutes before the first games kicked off, she toyed with changing her three lineups but decided to make no adjustments whatsoever.

Most Sundays Hunt watches games on TV while constantly checking her phone for DFS updates, but as this afternoon progressed she became so nervous that she gave her phone to Leslie and paced around the room. "Sometimes we'll have a few beers when we're watching football but we did three shots of tequila. I really needed to calm down. My heart was racing."

As it turned out, Geno Smith had his best game of the season, passing for 367 yards and three touchdowns. Lockett had a TD along with 128 receiving yards, in Seattle's 27-23 win over Los Angeles. The women had another shot of tequila followed by steaks ordered through DoorDash.

As for the bottom line, "amhunt2178" took first place in

the Milly Maker with one lineup and fourth place with another, for total winnings of $1.1 million. Three months later Hunt quit her job in logistics management at Amazon. "I wouldn't say I'm fully retired now," she explains, "I do a lot of investing." She still plays DFS and writes advice columns for the Dr. Roto site.

"To be honest with you, a lot of it has to be luck and having things fall in place the way you expect them to. I mean, nobody can predict who's going to do well. If that were the case, we'd all be rich."

As of this writing, Alisha Hunt is the only woman to have won a million-dollar prize in fantasy football.

♦ ♦ ♦

Though pro football continues to be viewed as a male-focused sport, the fact is women represent the fastest growing audience segment — for both the NFL and the fantasy football universe. Women and girls made up 46 percent of the NFL fan base (ages 8-plus) in the U.S., amounting to 84 million female fans, according to 2021 data from an SSRS Sports Poll. A 2024 survey conducted for the Fantasy Sports & Gaming Association shows that roughly 14 million women over age 18 participate in fantasy football.

Yet, as Matthew Berry observes, fantasy sports operate in "a fairly insular world." He believes it has gotten better, but recalls fantasy conferences not long ago where, "You'd go there and there were three women and two people of color. It was a lot of white men between 30 and 50."

Now, Berry told me, he sees a lot more women getting involved. "I get recognized these days by more women. I was at an event a couple of weeks ago where a woman came up to me and said she was a big fan. She let me know she's in four leagues, and she's the commissioner of two of them."

A study back in 2018 in the *Journal of Sport Management* found that men and women share three similar motives in fantasy games — "enjoy, enhance and socialize" — but two factors were deemed unique to female participants — "challenge and connect."

Connecting with other women who share an interest in fantasy football motivated Rachel Woodford (@tootsiepop6), a Vikings fan in Rochester, Minnesota, to create "Unwind," a female social media group. "We get on a Zoom call and we discuss fantasy football," she told me. "We discuss life, and it's just a hangout session. There's a good number of us women in the community. I think connection is really important, especially when we're a minority in a male-dominated sports industry."

Alisha Hunt is a regular attendee at Unwind sessions. "As far as DFS is concerned," she says, referring to her favorite format, "I don't feel like there's a huge female presence in it. Mostly all the women I interact with on the Unwind program, I would say 99 percent of them, are seasonal fantasy footballers. So I bring a different aspect to that group in itself by being a DFS player — a lot of our conversation is around strategies on the different types of platforms."

When Woodford reached out via Twitter for interested participants, she was surprised to find that several veteran commentators wished to join in, among them, Stephania Bell and Lindsay Rhodes.

Rhodes appeared for 12 years on NFL Network's "Total

Rachel Woodford with Scott Fish.

Access" show and more recently as co-host with Michael Fabiano on the "BLEAV Fantasy Football Show" podcast. She enthuses about "the special community" among women fantasy football players. "It's interesting how many people feel passionately about fantasy football. Everyone in the Unwind group is so kind and inclusive. It's just been a blast getting to know more people in this space."

Stephania Bell found her niche in football media by reporting on player injuries — an area of keen interest among fantasy managers and sports gamblers. A licensed physical therapist, board-certified orthopedic clinical specialist emeritus and certified strength and conditioning coach, she was hired by ESPN in 2008 and is best known as a host on the Sunday morn-

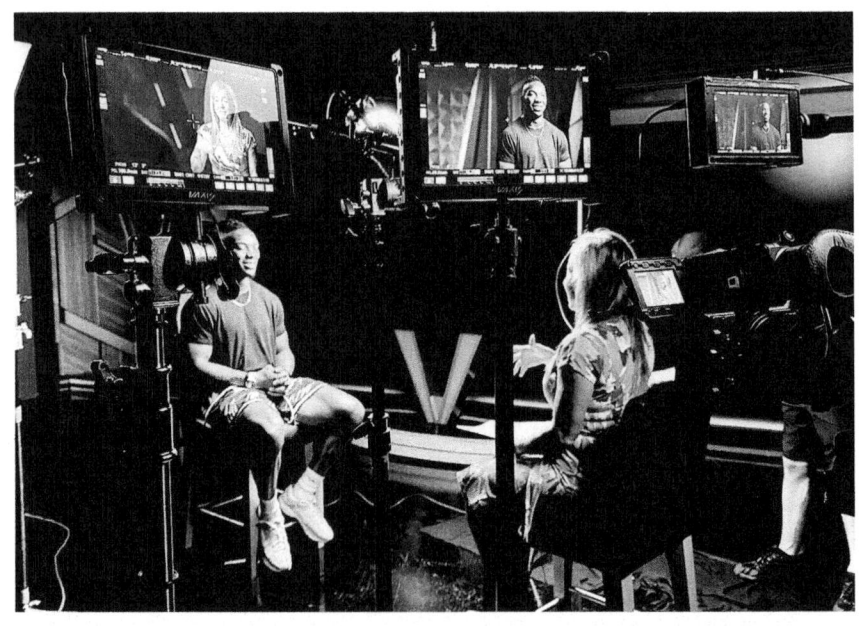

Stephania Bell sits down with the Falcons star Bijan Robinson.

ing series "Fantasy Football Now." She's a graduate of Princeton University with a degree in French Literature and earned a Master of Science in physical therapy from the University of Miami (Fla.).

"When I arrived at ESPN, it was the rare league that included female participants," Bell told me. "They often played in co-ed leagues where there were only one or two female members and they were typically recruited to fill out a league. The unspoken expectation was that they would be unskilled and therefore easier to defeat. However, many of these same women, aware of how they were perceived, made it their mission to learn and study as much as they could about the game which then translated to success. It also resulted in enjoyment of the game, which in turn led to continuing to play in subsequent years. Many of these earlier generation players would then go on to recruit more women into the fold and gradually that outreach has helped grow the numbers."

In 2024 Bell became the sixth recipient of the Matthew Berry "Game Changer" award and the first woman to receive the honor.

◆ ◆ ◆

Stacy Perez, a Tampa, Florida divorce attorney, was introduced to fantasy football by her dad at age 12, sitting at his side during drafting for a local seasonal league in 1996. "We took quarterback Brett Favre with our first pick," she recalls, "and even though my father bled popsicle orange for the Bucs, I became a huge Packer fan." (That season Green Bay won its third Super Bowl and Favre threw 39 touchdown passes, the most in his 20-year Hall of Fame career.)

At Fantasy Football Expo, from left, Faith Enes, Stacy Perez, Gemma Martinez, Lauren Carpenter, Britt Flinn, Kasey Royer, and Kelly Singh.

"Twenty-five years later I kind of got into it a little bit more than I previously had. I went from being more of a casual player to doing high stakes contests and actually traveling to do drafts. I have a cousin who runs a high stakes fantasy league out of Louisville, Kentucky and he got me into it. I met a ton of people and realized there's a lot more people out there that really enjoyed this just like I do.

"When I go to high stakes events I'm usually one of a small handful of women there. A lot of them are there to hang out with their husbands, they're not necessarily drafting themselves. In Kentucky, I'm probably the only single woman that goes. It was Rachel, having set up the Zoom chat and all of us being able to get to know each other. It opened my eyes to how there are so many women that are involved in fantasy in one way or another who you don't necessarily see when you go to live events."

Perez is now a commentator on several platforms. "The biggest challenge for me in fantasy football," she concedes, "is imposter syndrome: asking myself, 'Am I really qualified to do this?'" She also took the exam required to be a professional sports agent and hopes to sign some prospects to represent in the NFL. Her role model is Nicole Lynn, the acclaimed agent whose clients include Bijan Robinson of the Falcons and Jalen Hurts of the Eagles.

Following the Eagles Super Bowl appearance in 2023, Lynn negotiated a 5-year, $255 million contract for Hurts, with $179.4 million guaranteed. How did she come to represent him? As his college career was ending, she cold-messaged Hurts on Instagram: "Hey, just wondering if you've already chosen an agent?"

Lynn grew up in Tulsa, where she was a cheerleader, rugby player and a student of business management at the University of Oklahoma. At college she met her husband, Gabe, a cornerback for the Sooners who played briefly in the NFL. She returned to college to study law and interned with the NFL Players Association, then went to Norton Rose Fulbright, a Houston-based law firm. That led to an agent job at PlayersRep, followed by a position with Young Money APAA Sports, the agency owned by Lil Wayne. In 2021, she joined the Klutch Sports Group, becoming its President of Football Operations.

"As a woman in this industry, we're always fighting for a seat at the table," she said. "But it seems when we finally get there, we feel like we're not supposed to be at the table."

♦ ♦ ♦

Stacie Stern, first woman in the FSGA Hall of Fame.

In Boston on July 23, 2024, the Fantasy Sports & Gaming Association inducted the first woman, Stacie Stern, into its Hall of Fame, where she joined 25 men, including such notables as guru Matthew Berry and the inventor of the game, Bill Winkenbach. Candidates for the HOF must be considered a founder of the fantasy sports movement and therefore "active in the industry prior to 1990" [Stern did not begin in fantasy until 2001]. On her X page Stern unabashedly writes, "Some know me as First Lady of Fantasy Sports."

In honoring Stern, FSGA Chair Brandon Loeschner said, "I foresee a whole new generation of young women entering the industry because of Stacie's fearlessness in blazing her own trail."

Stern is a senior vice president at Underdog, where she is one of the leading voices lobbying in state capitals for fantasy sports. She was previously chair of FSGA, spent 15 years at Head2Head Sports and also worked at FanDuel for five years.

"With the explosive growth in fantasy sports, I'm most proud and excited about the sharp rise in participation by women," she said.

Growing up in Arizona, she was a college football fan and initially pursued a career in sports broadcasting. However, "I didn't like the way that I looked on camera. I was super critical." So she changed her major at Arizona State to political science. Hired by Head2Head in 2001 she had little awareness of fantasy sports but learned quickly. She told me that encouragement from Matthew Berry was pivotal as she mapped her course in the male-dominated fantasy sports field.

In 2015 Stern joined an all-female fantasy football league. "What I saw, even with my friends, was a real interest in sports and a desire to play fantasy sports, but they didn't know how to get started. Or they were nervous about playing against others who had played for years or worried about playing against men, because they didn't want to look stupid or make a bad decision. To me, that's something that is inherent in women that men don't typically suffer from."

She credits the NFL and other professional leagues for helping change the landscape for women. "They've worked to create an environment where women want to watch the games, whether it's with family members, spouses, partners or co-workers, whatever it is. And I think that was really a strategic and smart decision by the leagues because with viewership came an interest in fantasy sports. I think there are a lot more women playing today than those of us in the industry may have recognized for a long time, because they're doing it sort of quietly."

♦ ♦ ♦

"I know this seems insane," says Matthew Berry, "but I wonder if there's going to be an uptick in female fans because of the Taylor Swift effect. Taylor has a massive female audience. There are certainly a lot more women interested in the NFL and aware of the NFL because of Taylor Swift's interests. Just anecdotally, I have twin daughters, who are 12 years old, who could not care less about football and haven't cared about football, until this past year. They're both hardcore Swifties. Now, my daughters are watching football with me for the first time, because it was a game that Taylor Swift was going to be at. And they wanted to see it. Because they wanted to see, you know, shots of her in the audience. But they wanted to understand what Taylor's boyfriend did for a living."

♦ ♦ ♦

The Fantasy Football group on Reddit has over 2.6 million members. A women-only subgroup was organized by Bunny Peppers, called Women's Fantasy Football. "Fantasy football is still very male-dominated," she writes, "and I think we all agree it'd be awesome to be able to have mixed-sex leagues and there be no issues! But unfortunately there are still sex-based issues that stand in the way of that. WFF is intended to try to solve that issue. A woman who has gained confidence by being part of an all-women league is so much more likely to join a mixed-sex league in the future. Which is awesome!"

Asked about the differences in playing fantasy football in all-female leagues, she said, (1) "Knowing right off the bat that there's not going to be any sexism. I mean, there's basically no risk of it. No need to be on guard. (2) Generally just feeling more comfortable hanging out with other women. (3) Would often otherwise be the only woman in an all-male league, which makes you feel under the microscope. (4) Lots of first-timers, feels less intimidating when all the other players are women. (5) More in common in general, shared life experiences, being moms, that kinda thing."

There are countless other social media outlets, among them Women of Fantasy Football, whose YouTube channel and @WomenOf_FF postings on X, alerts female players to year-round drafts and high stakes contests. One of the founders, Faith Enes, explains, "Originally we had wanted to gather some women content creators but we recently decided that's not what our role is. That's not who we are. There are plenty of women content creators who are already creating for multiple sites. There doesn't need to be just one specific place where women gather. It's more important that women are in those places where it's mostly men, and we just promote the crap out of that."

The group's motto:

"Women of Fantasy Football exists to promote, support, and nurture women in sports so they know they can achieve what they dream. We believe that it's what's between your ears — not your legs — that matters most."

INSIDE FANTASY FOOTBALL /209

CHAPTER 13

Techno Touchdowns

Computers and AI have dramatically changed fantasy football...and the odds of winning.

In a much anticipated chess match in February 1996, the world champion Garry Kasparov faced IBM's Deep Blue, the most advanced chess-playing machine. Kasparov lost the first game but went on to win the match in Philadelphia, 4-2. It was humanity's proudest moment in competition pitting man vs. machine.

Fifteen months later in Manhattan, the two faced off again. In the intervening time engineers fixed a bug in Deep Blue's programming, while doubling its processing speed. Kasparov lost, stunning the chess community while boosting the hopes and spirits of the tech world.

Today, the notion of a human beating the best computer at chess is as far-fetched as a sprinter outracing a Bugatti. Is fantasy football heading down the same path? IBM, in partnership with ESPN, hopes so — as do dozens of tech companies and savvy individuals who are writing programs and developing tools to *game* the fantasy game. We know that in DFS football about 98 percent of the money is won by less than 2 percent of the participants. While the big winners are often smart, dedicated fans with lots of football knowledge, their edge almost always comes by using sophisticated computer tools.

As with the real game on the field, where coaches increasingly rely on analytics to determine their moves (the decision about whether to go for it on fourth down or punt being a prime example) fantasy managers are increasingly dependent on computer builds, simulations and statistical evaluations. With AI, fantasy football today faces the same challenge that the game of chess faced in '96.

"As a broke college kid, I discovered the thrill of potentially turning a small bet into thousands of dollars playing daily fantasy sports," writes Jacob Gibbs, an analyst at CBS Sports. "Fantasy football has come a long way as an industry since then, advanced analytics are more readily available than ever before. As someone who has been seeking out the edges of this space for a long time, I feel spoiled by the amount of information available in 2024.

"In seconds, I can find out what percentages of A.J. Brown's routes resulted in a target on plays when Jalen Hurts was blitzed. Within that split, I can filter out plays in which Dallas Goedert was on the field. I can filter it further to only include plays in which the Eagles were playing with a lead. The possibilities are endless!"

Rick Burton, the Syracuse University professor, told me, "I don't want to call it primitive but the version of fantasy sports, where we did it for fun, and we got our information from the newspaper, now looks quaint in the rearview mirror. As the sophistication of data has evolved, and even now, with the inclusion of artificial intelligence, I can say to a computer, 'who are the

Computers are at the heart of all sportsbook operations. In addition to its New York City headquarters, FanDuel opened a $15 million tech campus in Atlanta.

10 best players to draft?' Or, 'If I have these players on my team, and next week, I'm playing this guy, who should I play?' Where I used to think I knew football, now I'm forced to acknowledge that the machine knows football better than I do. And it's up to me whether I now want to use my own intuition, or I want to try and verify my intuition with available data from other sources."

I asked Burton if the quaintness of fantasy football, from the '90s or the early 2000s is going to be lost to technological advances.

"The short answer has to be yes, but I don't think it'll stop people from doing it. Everyone is always seeking a competitive advantage. The person using the computer is saying, 'Hey, this tool is available to me. And so I'm going to use it. The fact that you don't know how to use the tool, that's on you.'"

"It's only a skill game if you have the biggest bankroll and the best technology," John Sullivan, a former FanDuel consultant told ESPN. "That's the dirty little secret."

As David Bergman, the UConn professor who is one of fantasy football's most successful whales, sees it, "There is a wide range of players. Some are more intuitive, some are more analytical players, and there are people who fall within that spectrum. I am definitely more of an analytics person — almost all of it done with AI, machine learning and optimization.

"I think the best of the best combine what the state of the art is as far as analytics together with some knowledge of sports."

Peter Overzet sees an increasing role for AI, especially in DFS. "That's where the most money can be won, with DraftKings putting up million dollar prizes. That means it's going to attract people who are the sharpest. It's now par for the course that you need to be using simulations to win consistently in DFS, but no one's building a proprietary model to win their 12-person home League, right? The juice isn't worth the squeeze. But the full length season is such a chaotic animal that a lot of the giga-brains right now say, 'I can't sim out a full season, we don't even know how to do it.' But as we know, with all of this stuff, the technology will probably get there."

Alisha Hunt, fantasy football's top-earning woman, believes, "It's unfortunate that a lot of DFS action is going just straight computer which, to me, takes the fun out of it. I find it enjoyable to actually go in and pick. I mean, yes, I will run an optimizer, I will run some sims and look at what they're thinking. But you have to take a lot of factors into consideration that I don't believe a computer can do.

"Even if I won another million dollars, I would still like to handle my picks or my lineups. But with AI being such a big thing and coming into play, it's going to change the whole game."

◆ ◆ ◆

Back in 2017, Bergman wrote a research paper titled "Surviving a National Football League Survivor Pool." (In such contests, a participant must pick a winning team for one of the NFL games played in a given week. If this team loses, the participant is eliminated from the pool. If it wins, the participant selects a team to win in the next week, but cannot choose any team he previously selected.)

"We were able to build a predictive model to estimate the win probability for each team in each game — starting for any point of the season and lasting throughout the season," said Bergman. "In any given week, we can deduce a relatively accurate prediction for the probability that any team will win in that week. For future weeks, however, the probabilities will change as the season progresses, sometimes substantially."

That same year, a Columbia University professor, Raghav Singal, conducted a research project (with the help of Martin Haugh of Imperial College Business School) the goal of which was to beat FanDuel in DFS for the 2017 season. Their paper, published two years later, was titled "How to Play Fantasy Sports Strategically (and Win)." After straining to understand their 52 pages of equations and scientific jargon, I decided to track down Singal, now at Dartmouth, for a simpler summary.

Citing his background in finance, Singal explained, "I thought finance and fantasy sports came together for someone who's interested in doing sports analytics, but also is well versed in portfolio optimization. In the end, you're essentially optimizing a portfolio of athletes." Interestingly, having grown up in India, Singal didn't even know the rules of American football when he began his project and had never played fantasy sports.

The essence of his research was to identify patterns in large-field contests, such as those most popular in DFS. If, for example, you determined how the entrants in FanDuel's competition reacted to the play of, say, quarterback Matthew Stafford, then you could create models that would predict how the field would react to another quarterback in a subsequent week who faced a similar situation. "The underlying assumption is that if the factors are the same, then the opponents will behave the same way."

The researchers played with real money, but only tiny sums. With an initial investment of $50 in Week 1 (one dollar for each of 50 lineups) the men lost everything. In Week 2 they kicked in another $30. By the end of Week 17 they had turned a profit of $200 (which they donated to charity). Singal points out that he would have fared even better had he made late lineup changes — for instance, swapping a player on Sunday morning based on news of an injury — but he did not. The best week that season for the model was a finish in 138th place among 178,000 entrants. Unlike David Bergman, Singal did not opt to monetize his research and continue playing fantasy football for fun or profit.

Raghav Singal researched DFS at Columbia.

The researchers concluded that the more lineups a savvy player can enter in a DFS contest — up to 150 — the more effective models and algorithms become. "Think of it this way: If you give more decision-making ability to sophisticated players, and by that I mean deciding about 150 lineups as opposed to one lineup, they can really leverage that. So, with contests with so many lineups it's really about skill, whereas if it's only one lineup, I think the rule of luck might still come in."

I offered a counter argument. "I wonder if the operative word is luck," I said, "or if a fantasy player like myself might actually call that the highest level of skill, because if I'm playing against opponents who can only put in one lineup each, then I would think that now their computers don't do them as much good. And so my skill in competing with them — because I know who the good players are, I know what the weather is, I know what this coach tends to do in road games versus home games, etc. — all these variables that I consider part of my skill set would come into play more if I were playing one lineup against one lineup, right?"

"I would agree with that," he said.

◆ ◆ ◆

My thoughts notwithstanding, it's clear that in the future AI will provide a significant edge for those fantasy players able to afford it.

ESPN has partnered with IBM to utilize generative AI technology in its fantasy football app, available to some 11 million participants on the ESPN fantasy football site. The system analyzes both player stats and written reports from local beat writers and others covering NFL news, to produce "waiver grades" and "trade grades." As IBM vice president Noah Syken told me, "The structured data lets you pair it up with the unstructured data, the written words, and distill all of that data for fans and give them a new tool so they can be better players in fantasy football."

Syken was reluctant to say what IBM engineers are working on behind the scenes, but he did note that in private, unpublished simulations, its computers have fared well in predicting NFL outcomes.

Dan Bohm, ESPN's Director of Product Development, says, "AI is the new hotness. One of the things we're focused on at ESPN is how can we make (fantasy football) easier for people and more fun and less like homework. That's where some of the new technology comes in."

Bohm told me that ESPN's partnership with IBM is aimed at making fantasy players smarter managers. "We're the largest fantasy football provider, so we have fans who are more sophisticated as well as some who are less so. One of our challenges is figuring out how to serve those users who want to go really deep (with AI) while not ailienating those who don't. We're working on creating personalized recaps for seasonal leagues, using technology to make the game more enjoyable."

♦ ♦ ♦

In conducting interviews for this book I made a point of asking people in the fantasy football community about the impact of technology. Here's a sample of what I heard.

Andrew Sears, President, FantasyPros:

"AI is essentially changing everything. So that includes the way that we work, communicate, collaborate, and create as well. So we definitely feel that if we don't embrace AI, then we'll be at a disadvantage. Someone in the fantasy space is going to drive innovation by using AI."

Jake Ciely, lead fantasy writer, *The Athletic*:

"I think it can be good and bad in different ways. On the good side is what we were seeing with DFS. That's where you get the most optimization by running a simulation 1,000 times. The bad side of it is that you get potentially a little bit less personality if people are just consuming information. There are a lot of personalities I know in the industry, and if AI eliminates even 10 percent of their jobs, I worry about fantasy sports becoming dehumanized."

Pat Kerrane, analyst and million-dollar winner:

"Peer-to-peer games trend toward being more efficient, and AI will likely speed up that process. As a player in that game, I don't want that. I want the game to be inefficient, so I can beat the game. But while it may become harder to take down the top prizes, I'm not worried about fantasy. Fundamentally, people play fantasy because it's a lot of fun. I don't see AI changing that."

Rick Wolf, analyst and founding member of the FSGA:

"The athletes play on the field and there's no way to perfectly predict them with a computer. We tried it over and over again, mostly with baseball, because we thought baseball was the most predictable. And we went through model after model and we couldn't get close enough to where we would feel comfortable with saying we can predict with any accuracy what players were going to do. With the unpredictability of humans in general, it's almost impossible to have those models work out. Now, for people who are using enough variance, and publishing 150 lineups at a time, what we're finding is that so many people are doing it that it's getting much more competitive."

Matthew Berry, NBC analyst and owner of Fantasy Life:

"I don't think AI is causing major shifts in what the game is. Ultimately, the game is still, at the end of the day, played by people, played by your friends, your classmates, your relatives, your work colleagues. It's a social game that you play with people you have a relationship with and AI is not gonna replace that. Will AI make research better? Can it improve the techniques? I think all those things are very true. But to mix sports metaphors, I think we're still in the first inning of AI."

◆ ◆ ◆

Due in large part to technology, the game that started in Bill Winkenbach's basement has grown so much and embraced so many different formats that it's increasingly imprecise to label all of it "fantasy football." High-stakes DFS, most notably, has become a virtual battle of bots. Even players who insist that they make their lineups "by hand" are usually relying on computers for the underlying data along with simulations. Basic recreational redraft leagues remain removed from that world, but many of the experts I spoke with note that computer software is already at hand to analyze drafting in real time and then to create the most favorable lineups during the season.

Beyond the weights and measures of technology, the fantasy field is even more vulnerable to its conflation with gambling. It was the Deep Throat character in "All the President's Men" who popularized the phrase, "Follow the money." And it was the character Rod Tidwell in "Jerry Maguire" who demanded, "Show me the money!" Both could easily have been talking about fantasy football. As soon as the U.S. Supreme Court ruled in 2018 that states could authorize sports gambling pretty much as they wished, everything changed in fantasy sports. The fantasy operators became sportsbooks and the sportsbooks opened fantasy platforms. Media outlets embraced gambling and packaged it with fantasy contests. And pro leagues, including the NFL, went from being fierce gambling opponents to gung ho gaming advocates.

This is not to say sports gambling shouldn't be legal. What should concern the fantasy sports community is the way the activities are overlapping. The raging debate between DraftKings and FanDuel vs. Underdog and PrizePicks about whether pick'em games should be regulated as fantasy or gambling underscores where things are headed. Underdog and PrizePicks, as we discussed earlier, insist that such prop contests are just another form of fantasy competition. But who are they kidding?

In my Foreword I briefly mentioned "obsession" and "addiction" when it comes to fantasy sports. To me, spending way too much time analyzing lineup decisions and reading the opinions of dozens of experts and checking the phone at stoplights to avoid missing a play — that's an obsession. Jumping into a best ball tournament right after you've finished the last one, filling out 150 DFS lineups and then looking for another link so you can run 150 more, and making click after click to place your pick'em bets — that seems more like an addiction.

Throughout these pages many folks have used words like "relationships" and "camaraderie" and "fraternity" to describe what fantasy football means to them. Another group, however, explains the appeal with terms such as "action" and "sweat." I'm sure there's room for both. I only hope that corporate greed doesn't wind up spoiling what for many of us is a really cool thing.

I've come to appreciate what fun it is to be a part of a gigantic community of over 50 million fantasy football players, each of whom is an expert.

APPENDIX

Fantasy Football Lingo

Tyreek Hill of the Dolphins figures to be near the top among wide receivers in 2024 fantasy drafts.

Action: The amount of money a user has in play during a specific period.

aDot (Average depth of target): The number of air yards the football travels per pass attempt.

ADP (Average Draft Position): A ranking of NFL players based on where they are being selected in fantasy drafts on average.

Air yards: The distance a pass travels in the air before it is caught or incomplete.

Auction draft: A type of fantasy draft in which owners roster players by bidding. Each owner receives a budget to spend on players, and each player goes to the highest bidder. Owners take turns introducing an opening bid for a player.

Bell-cow RB: A running back who tends to get the majority of snaps on all downs on his NFL team.

Bench players: Players on your roster whom you choose to not start. They receive no points for their performances while on your bench.

Best ball league: A type of competition in which the rostered player with the best points at each position counts towards your weekly total.

Best ball scoring: A format in which managers don't set weekly lineups. The score is determined by taking the highest point total at each lineup spot. (Example: Your roster has three QBs. The one with the highest fantasy point total in a given week goes toward your score; the other two are ignored.)

Breakout: A player who improves significantly, rising above projections.

Bring it back: In a stacked DFS lineup, one or more players from the opposing team are selected. (Example: You stack Chiefs QB Patrick Mahomes with WR Rashee Rice and TE Travis Kelce in an NFL game against the Texans. You bring it back with Nico Collins on the assumption that if KC is scoring a lot, the opponents are too.)

Blind bidding: A system used in some leagues to protect against cheating. Bids are submitted on players without knowing the bids from other teams. After all bids are in, the high bidder gets the player.

Boom-or-bust: An inconsistent player prone to widely varying weekly scores. (See "floor" and "ceiling.")

Bust: A player who does not live up to expectations, via poor play or injury.

Buy-in: The cost of entering a contest.

Bye week: For each NFL team, the week in the schedule when they do not play.

Cash games: DFS contests in which at least half the field gets paid. (Examples: 50/50, double-up, head-2-head.)

Ceiling: The high end of expectations for a player's fantasy points on a given week or season. (See: "floor.")

Chalk: In DFS play, a very popular NFL player, taken by many entrants.

Cheat sheet: A drafting tool ranking NFL players in order of their projected fantasy point expectations, based on league settings.

Correlate: Matching players on the same NFL team in a fantasy roster, for instance a quarterback and his top receiver.

Combine: A event with a series of fitness tests that help scouts from NFL teams evaluate amateur athletes — a highly anticipated prelude to the annual NFL draft.

Comeback: After making a pick in a snake-style draft, the "comeback" is when the draft works its way back to your next pick.

Commissioner: In private leagues, the person responsible for maintaining rosters and stats, running the draft, collecting entry fees and generally keeping things running smoothly.

Contrarian: Selecting players or making roster moves that are contrary to the most common or "chalky" moves.

Cut: To remove a player from your roster. (Also "drop" or "release.")

Daily Fantasy Sports (DFS): fantasy contests played in one day or a very short duration.

DEF: A team's defense.

Deep League: A league with more than 12 owners and/or rosters that are larger than normal. Such leagues wind up with fewer players in the free agent pool.

Depth chart: NFL rosters showing the ranking of players at each position — the starter and the backups.

Devy (developmental) league: A format where college players are drafted and held until they reach the NFL. (Created by Scott Fish.)

Differential: A low-owned NFL player with considerable upside potential.

DNP (Did not practice): An indication that an NFL player did not participate in team drills on a given day.

Double-tap: When a fantasy owner with back-to-back picks takes players at the same position.

Doubtful (D): An NFL designation indicating a player has about a 25 percent chance of playing in the current week.

Draft: The selection of NFL players in a fantasy league, usually conducted as an "auction draft" or "snake" draft.

DST: A team's defense plus its special teams.

Dynasty league: A fantasy football format in which managers maintain their rosters year over year.

Dynasty draft: An annual draft held by a dynasty league's managers to select players from the incoming NFL rookie class and any other un-rostered players.

ECR (Expert Consensus Ranking): The combined average ranking given a player by a pool of experts.

Enabler: A low-cost player who allows a fantasy manager to afford more expensive players.

Exposure: The measure of how much a particular player is rostered by a participant over the course of an event or tournament. (If, for example, you have Josh Allen on three of your 12 best ball teams, you have 25% exposure.)

FAAB (Free Agent Acquisition Budget): A waiver wire method where each team owner is given a budget for the season that is used for blind bidding on players in the free agent pool.

Fade: To stay away from a certain player.

Flex: A spot in a starting lineup that can be used for more than one type of position player, most often running backs, wide receivers and tight ends. (Some leagues allow an owner to use a quarterback in the flex slot.)

Floor: The low end of expectations for a player's fantasy points on a given week or season. (See: "ceiling.")

FPPG: Fantasy points per game.

Free agent: An NFL player not currently on any manager's roster. If the league has a waiver system, free agents are players who have cleared waivers.

Freeroll: A DFS game offered by fantasy platforms that allows a free entry for a chance to win cash prizes, usually designed to attract new customers to the fantasy site.

Game script: The expected flow of an NFL game, used by fantasy managers to determine player value. (Example: If the Chiefs are expected to grab a big early lead against the Raiders, then Kansas City might be expected to do more running later in the game while Las Vegas would turn to more passing.)

Go-to WR: The wide receiver who is the primary target option for an NFL team. Sometimes referred to as the "alpha" receiver.

GPP (guaranteed prize pool): A DFS contest in which the prizes are guaranteed regardless of whether the maximum number of participants is reached.

Green zone: A term developed by television, it's the area between the line of scrimmage and the first down marker.

Grinder: A player who "grinds out" many entries.

Guillotine league: A format in which the lowest scoring team is eliminated each week and its players become free agents. The process continues until only one team remains.

Half-PPR: The fantasy football scoring format in which pass receptions are counted as 0.5 points.

Hand build: Creating a fantasy lineup without computer assistance.

Handcuff: Rostering a stud player's real-life backup, usually an RB, to protect a fantasy roster in the event the starter is injured or suspended.

Hero RB: A draft strategy in which a running back is selected first but additional RB picks are delayed until later rounds, thus the "hero" label for the early selection.

H2H (Head-to-Head): A fantasy format in which one team competes directly against another in a given week.

IDP (Individual Defensive Player): A departure from the team defense approach, some leagues require each owner to start individual defensive linemen (DL), linebackers (LB) and defensive backs (DB). The number of starters and the scoring settings for these positions varies by league.

IR (Injured Reserve): An option in some fantasy leagues allowing an injured player to be placed on IR so that his roster spot is freed for a replacement. (Not to be confused with the NFL's official IR designation for injured players.)

Keeper league: A type of fantasy league in which each owner is allowed to retain a set number of NFL players from the previous season's roster.

Late swap: A feature on many platforms that allows lineup changes on late games even after early games are underway.

Lock: The time when final lineups must be submitted for fantasy competition. ("Lock" sometimes also refers to a player who is very likely to succeed.)

Manager: The person in control of all decisions (drafting, weekly lineups, trades, free agency, etc.) for a fantasy team.

Mock draft: A practice draft used to refine drafting strategy and gauge where NFL players are likely to be selected in actual fantasy drafts.

Multiplier: A prize structure in DFS in which winners multiply their entry fee. As multipliers go up the odds become larger and the payout increases.

Naked pick: An NFL player selected for a fantasy roster without any correlation to another player on that NFL team, for instance, taking a quarterback without anyone on his real-life team to whom he might throw.

NFL draft: A seven-round event held every April in which NFL teams select top college football prospects.

Optimizer: Computer programs used to create DFS lineups for multiple entry contests.

Out (O): An official NFL designation for a player who will not participate in the current week.

Overlay: The amount of money a DFS platform loses when the guaranteed prize pool is greater than the sum of all entry fees. (Example: If the guaranteed prize pool is $50,000 and the entry fees total $45,000 the overlay is $5,000.)

Picking at the turn: A team that picks first or last in a snake-style draft, thus making two picks in a row during the draft process — the last pick of a round and the first pick of the following round.

Pickup: A player you added to your fantasy roster.

Pirate league: A format in which a winning manager gets to select a player from the losing manager's roster.

Platoon: Typically referring to an NFL team backfield in which volume is distributed equitably between multiple running backs.

Player pool: The entire group of available NFL players for a fantasy league.

Power rankings: A ranking system using multiple criteria to grade teams or players.

PPR (Point Per Reception): In some leagues, owners earn a fantasy point for each reception their players produce during a game. In these leagues, wide receivers and pass-catching running backs are much more valuable than in standard leagues.

Probable (P): A designation on the NFL injury report that a player has about a 75 percent chance of playing this week.

Projections: Statistical estimations of player's value in a week or over a full season. It attempts to guess the total stats for a player given a certain timeframe. Also found often on cheat sheets. (See: Cheat Sheet.)

Qualifier: A contest in which the winners gain access to another contest, usually for a larger prize pool. Qualifiers are most often used for large-scale daily fantasy tournaments.

Quarterback Room: In real life, the meeting room for quarterbacks at the team's facility (also WR room, RB room, etc.). In fantasy football it has become shorthand in referring to the group of players an NFL team has at each skill position.

Questionable (Q): A designation on the NFL injury report that a player has about a 50 percent chance of playing this week.

QB1, QB2: In ranking player value, a QB1 is a quarterback who ranks as a top-10 option, while a QB2 is ranked from 11-20 at the position. The third tier would be QB3, from 21-30. Similar rankings would be used for wide receivers (WR), running backs (RB) and tight ends (TE).

Rake: The percentage of money that the operating platform takes from entry fees as its profit. Usually about 10 or 12 percent but sometimes as high as 16 percent. (In conventional sports wagering, the "vigorish" or "vig" or "juice.")

RBBC (Running back by committee): A strategy used increasingly by NFL teams to play two or more RBs, dividing the work in the backfield and relying less on a single RB or "bell cow."

Redraft leagues: Unlike keeper and dynasty leagues, redraft leagues make all players available to be drafted at the start of each new fantasy football season.

Red zone: The area inside the opponent's 20-yard line.

ROI: "Return on Investment," in reference to how a player performs relative to where they were selected in a fantasy draft.

Room: As in, "quarterback room" or "wide receiver room" — a recently popularized reference to the group of players at a particular position on an NFL team, coined because players and coaches have strategy meetings in separate rooms based on position.

Roster: The players that make up a fantasy football team.

Roto (Rotisserie): An older term referring to fantasy sports. (The name comes from the meeting place of an early fantasy baseball league whose members, led by writer Daniel Okrent, met at La Rotisserie Francaise restaurant in New York City. Okrent later said most of the gatherings were actually at P.J. Moriarity's.) Also used to describe a form of league play in which teams do not play one another individually but play against the entire field each week and earn points based on their league rankings in each statistical category.

Roto Scoring: Comes from Rotisserie Baseball. A scoring system where fantasy teams are scored in multiple stat categories. In each category, each team gets one point plus one point for each other team that it beats in that category.

Salary cap draft: A draft in which managers use a predetermined budget to build a team by bidding on players.

Scoring: Abbreviations include: TD = Touchdown; Yds = Yards; FG = Field Goal; XP = Extra Point; INT = Interception; Pts = Points.

Sharpe ratio: An investment metric applied to fantasy football telling you how much extra return you're getting for taking on the amount of risk you're getting in selecting a player.

Shark: A highly experienced, expert fantasy player. (In sports wagering, a "sharp.")

Simulation (Sims): The use of computer programs to predict how a game will go. There is even wagering on the Madden game simulations.

Sleeper: An NFL player who could have a breakout season but may be undervalued in fantasy drafts or a player who is just not well known.

Snake draft: A draft type that reverses order after each round. Also known as a "serpentine draft." (Example: In a 10-team league, the 10th position would have the first pick in the second round, as the draft snakes forward and back.)

Snipe: In drafts, when the player you plan to select is taken just before it's your turn.

Sortino ratio: As defined by the fantasy player Sackreligious, "it's a metric that can capture a player's floor/ceiling combo in one neat number. Players with a high Sortino ratio aren't boom/bust. They boom more often (or boom bigger) and bust less frequently (or less severely)."

Square: A novice or recreational fantasy player — the opposite of a "shark."

Stack: Setting a lineup to combine more than one player from a single NFL team, usually a QB and one or more of his WRs. (In "game stacking" you would add one or more players from the opposing team as well: "bringing it back.")

Standard scoring: A system where you receive points for yardage gained (as in 1 point for every 25 passing yards) in addition to the points awarded in a basic scoring system.

Starters: The players in your fantasy lineup.

Start/Sit: Advice, usually offered by experts, about which players to start and which to bench each week.

Stream (or Streaming): Instead of rostering a dedicated starter week-to-week, an owner might prefer to stream a position by picking up free agents or waiver picks. (Example: Instead of drafting a kicker, an owner opts to pick up a different kicker each week based on matchup.)

Strength of schedule (SOS): An estimate, usually by experts, of the degree of difficulty faced by an NFL team or individual player for the remainder of the season.

Stud: An NFL player who has proven himself to be a top-scoring fantasy player at his position.

Superflex: A flex roster spot that allows an owner to start an extra QB, in addition the usual RB, WR or TE options of a flex spot. (See: "flex.")

Survivor leagues: Participants must pick a winning team for one of the NFL games that are played in a given week. If this team loses, the participant is eliminated from the pool. If this team wins, the participant selects a team to win in the next week, but cannot choose any team he has previously selected.

Swap: The process of adjusting your fantasy lineup between early and late Sunday games based on how you are doing or how your opponents are doing.

Sweat: The tense moments in competition, when the final plays might determine the outcome.

Targets: The number of times a player is the intended recipient of a pass, regardless of whether the pass is complete.

TE1, TE2: A TE1 is a tight end who ranks as a top-10 option, while a TE2 is ranked from 11-20 at the position.

TD-only: Fantasy football scoring format that only awards points for touchdowns, not yardage.

TE-premium scoring: A fantasy football scoring format in which tight ends receive a higher value for receptions than the other positions.

Team position: Instead of earning points from one specific player at a position, you earn points from every player at that position on a particular NFL team. Thus, if a team uses, say, two QBs in a game, you get the points earned by both.

Third-round reversal: A snake-style draft with a twist. In a third-round reversal draft, the order in which teams select in Round 1 is reversed for Round 2, with Round 3 following in the same order as Round 2. Round 4 and each subsequent round revert to the typical serpentine process.

Ticket: Awarded on platforms such as DraftKings, giving the fantasy player entree to a larger tournament.

Tier: When ranking players based on expected value, players of similar worth are grouped on a single tier.

Total Points: A format in which each manager competes against everyone in the league, not just a single opponent each week. Typically, you would pay some amount to everyone ahead of you and collect from everyone behind.

Touches: The times during a game that a player handles the ball — by taking a handoff, catching a pass, receiving a kick or recovering a fumble.

Touts: Experts who give advice on drafting, lineups, strategy, etc.

Trade: Swapping certain players in accordance with rules of a fantasy league.

Train: In DFS contests, entering the same lineup multiple times.

Transaction: A roster change. Some leagues have a transaction fee. See: Cut or Drop, Pickup and Trade.

Triple-Up: Like a double up or 50/50, except winners win triple the entry fee of the contest and have to beat more than two-thirds of the players.

Undroppables: Elite players who, according to fantasy league rules, cannot be cut or dropped during the season.

Vampire league: A format in which everyone but one person drafts. At the end of the draft the vampire builds a team based on waivers. Then each week if the vampire wins, they can take any player from the opposing team and add it to their own.

Volume: For quarterbacks, volume refers to pass attempts. For running backs and receivers, volume refers to touches. In fantasy football, "volume is king" is a common refrain.

Vulture: An NFL player who gets the points for, say, a one-yard TD plunge, after contributing little to the scoring drive. (Example: When Gus Edwards played for the Ravens he occasionally entered the game just to make a short TD run, thus "vulturing" fantasy points from other players.)

Watchlist: A feature on some fantasy platforms that enables managers to monitor the performance of certain players without actually rostering them.

Whale: In DFS, a player who enters many contests and spends a lot of money.

Waivers: Players cut in most leagues do not immediately become free agents and available to any team. Instead, they go on waivers for a day or more. While on waivers, owners can make a waiver claim for the recently released player. Usually, the claiming team with the highest waiver priority gets the player.

Waiver order: Each team begins the season with a waiver priority number that is most commonly the reverse of its draft spot. So, the team that had the No. 1 pick in a 12-team draft would start off with the No. 12 waiver priority. Conversely, the team that had the 12th and final pick of the first round would have the No. 1 priority. Once an owner uses his or her waiver priority to successfully add a player, their priority number falls to the bottom of the league.

Waiver priority: A specific order of who gets a player signed off waivers if they are claimed by more than one fantasy owner. It's established before the season.

WR1, WR2, WR3: In a 10-team league, a WR1 is a top-10 wide receiver, a WR2 is ranked from 11-20, and a WR3 is ranked 21-30.

YAC: "Yards after contact" when referring to a rusher. It can also be "yards after catch" when referring to a receiver's additional yards gained after securing possession of a pass.

YPA: "Yards per attempt" for a quarterback, calculated by dividing the total passing yards by the number of pass attempts.

YPC: "Yards per carry" for a rusher, or "yards per catch" for a receiver. (It can also be referred to as YPR, "yards per reception.")

Zero-RB strategy: When an owner opts to "fade" or avoid the RB position early in the draft. Instead, the owner will select WRs early in the draft. More common in leagues where there are three starting WR slots (instead of two) and one or more flex slots.

Zero-WR strategy: A drafting methodology in which a team manager avoids the wide receiver position in the early rounds of a draft.

3RR: "3rd Round Reversal," allowing the bottom of the draft order to start Round 3 after also starting Round 2. Used to balance draft opportunities in larger leagues.

NOTES

Setting out to write about fantasy football seemed almost like a vacation — covering a topic I enjoyed and thought I knew a lot about. The task turned out to be like unraveling a ball of yarn. The more I learned, the more I realized how much there was to know. After all, we're talking about an activity enjoyed by millions of Americans, driving dozens of giant companies, with billions of dollars at stake. Whew.

I wound up interviewing over 80 people, some multiple times. I don't want to list them all here (their names are sprinkled liberally on the preceding pages) but I do wish to give each my sincere thanks. That said, as George Orwell's "Animal Farm" notes, "All pigs are equal, but some are more equal than others." So I offer special shout-outs to a few folks, starting with Emil Kadlec, the fantasy sports pioneer, whose encyclopedic memory is a treasured resource. Emil's most notable project was creating a library of over 30 video interviews with "Fantasy Sports Pioneers." It's on the Fantasy Nation site at:

https://fantasynation.com/fantasy-sports-pioneers/

Speaking of pioneers, two in particular were kind enough to share their earliest memories — Gerald Winkenbach, whose father "Wink" invented fantasy football, and Stan Heeb, commissioner and a member of the GOPPPL group since 1974.

The Fantasy Sports & Gaming Association is a repository for much valuable information and two of its leading members, Rick Wolf and Paul Charchian, were especially gracious in helping — and correcting — me. While the FSGA focuses on the business side, the Fantasy Sports Writers Association keeps tabs on the content providers. (Note to self: Please stop using "content" to describe writing and commentary as if it's so many pounds of baloney on the butcher's scale.) Andy Behrens of Yahoo Sports is the president of the group and was enormously helpful to me.

And, of course, there's The Talented Mr. Roto, Matthew Berry. If there was a stat for "Number of Mentions" by people thanking someone for career guidance and help, Berry would get top honors — and I'd be among the grateful.

On the editorial side, chief researcher and production manager Brian Courrejou was a beacon, as he is on all our projects. Copy editing help was provided by Bonnie Weinstein, with an assist from her husband Joel. Also, my son, Danny Funt, and my friend and colleague Clarence Fanto.

◆ ◆ ◆

PHOTO CREDITS:

Pg 19, 31, 202 - Bob Lung
Pg 37 - John Thorn
Pg 53, 55, 57 - Emil Kadlec
Pg 63, 101 - Rick Wolf
Pg 72, 93 - Paul Charchian
Pg 105 - National Football League
Pg 109 - Detroit Lions
Pg 121 - Houston Texans
Pg 125 - (composite) NBC Sports
Pg 140 - Jake Ciely
Pg 149 - Peter Overzet
Pg 151 - Austin Ekeler Foundation
Pg 175, 181 - Michael Cohen
Pg 193 - Stacie Stern
Pg 196 - Alisha Hunt
Pg 217 - Raghav Singal
Pg 223 - Miami Dolphins

INDEX

Adams, Devante, 21-23, 106, 159,
Aikman, Troy, 185
Alberth, Andy, 154
Alito, Samuel, 94
Allan, Ian, 68, 69
Ambrosius, Greg, 94
Anderson, Steve, 41, 43
Bajaria, Bela, 107
Banaszak, Pete, 58
Baumgartner, Brian, 163, 165
Barkley, Saquon, 119, 157
Behrens, Andy, 120, 127-130, 141, 160, 168,
Bell, Jarrett, 107
Bell, Stephania, 136, 199, 200
Bergman, David, 177-180, 214, 215
Berry, Matthew, 17, 30, 31, 63, 95, 99, 100, 111, 112, 115, 125, 130-136, 143, 149, 156, 160, 165, 166, 173, 186, 197, 198, 200, 203, 205, 206, 220
Blanda, George, 53, 55,
Blum, Bob, 51
Bond, Joe, 144
Bonn, Amanda, 104
Brown, Jim, 50, 56, 62
Buck, Joe, 185
Buckley, Andy, 163
Buckley, William, 36, 37
Buffett, Jimmy, 134, 135
Burton, Rick, 36, 38, 212, 213,
Bush, Jeb, 89, 90
Canon, Terry, 113
Cao, Youda, 182-184
Carmona, Phil, 52
Casebolt, Ralph, 52

Charchian, Paul, 66, 71, 73, 92, 93, 117, 118,
Charpentier, Cliff, 65, 66, 67, 70, 73, 81
Christie, Chris, 90, 91, 93
Ciely, Jake, 138-141, 143, 219
Cohen, Michael, 175, 180-182
Cruz, Jose, 178
Cuban, Mark, 92, 93, 115,
Daniels, Jayden, 159
Dodd, Mason, 121, 188
Diggs, Stefon, 121
Ditka, Mike, 50
Downey, Robert, 165
Duggan, Dan, 156
Eccles, Nigel, 84, 85,
Ekeler, Austin, 151, 158, 159, 160, 189
Etienne, Travis, 155, 156
Evans, Chris, 165
Fabiano, Michael, 199
Fallon, Jimmy, 166, 167
Feldman, Marty, 50
Ferrara, Jerry, 170, 171
Ferrell, Will, 161, 168
Fish, Scott, 149, 171-173, 199
Fitzmaurice, Pat, 141
Florio, Michael, 105
Funston, Brandon, 132,
Gamboa, David, 117, 122, 123
Gamson, William, 61
Gibbs, Jacob, 212
Gifford, Frank, 16, 50
Glace, George, 52
Goff, Jared, 115
Goodell, Roger, 27, 28, 95, 106, 107

Grant, Marcas, 105, 158
Greene, Jeff, 167
Grogan, Dan, 69
Grogan, Kelly, 69, 70
Hamilton, Tom, 39
Hamlin, Damar, 185
Hamm, Jon, 170, 171
Hanson, Scott, 88, 180
Harbaugh, Jim, 22
Harmon, Matt, 159
Harstad, Adam, 30
Haugh, Martin, 215
Hawkins, Trip, 44,
Heeb, Stan, 60, 61,
Holt, Lester, 89
Holt, Samantha, 193
Hsu, Will, 21
Hughes, Patrick, 73, 74
Hunt, Alisha, 195-198, 214
Hunt, Lamar, 26
Huntley, Tyler, 22
Hurley, Chad, 133
Jacobs, Josh, 118
James, LeBron, 133
Jay-Z, 165, 166
Jefferson, Justin, 106
Johns, Pau, 69
Kadlec, Emil, 113, 114,
Kalish, Matt, 85, 86
Kane, Tom, 65, 67
Kasparov, Garry, 211
Kerrane, Pat, 185-189, 220
Khan, Tony, 133
Kim, David, 141
King, Matt, 87
Kittle, George, 106
Krasinski, John, 163
Koerner, Sean, 143, 144
Landry, Cejaay, 145, 146
Leach, Jim, 82, 83
Legend, John, 133
Levine, Jeremy, 114, 115, 122,

Levitan, Adam, 120, 184,
LaPorta, Sam, 109
Liberman, Paul, 85
Loeschner, Brandon, 204
Lohia, Ankit, 179
Love, Jordan, 120
Loza, Jesus, 151
Lozano, Guillermo, 165
Lung, Bob, 30, 31, 113,
Lynn, Nicole, 202, 203
Madden, John, 43-45, 54, 55, 74, 154,
Mahomes, Patrick, 118
Mantle, Mickey, 16
Marino, Dan, 69, 72
McCaffrey, Christian, 33, 44, 119,
Meyers, Seth, 166
Moon, Warren, 66, 67
Moore, Ryan, 85
Mousalimas, Andy, 55, 56, 57, 58, 59, 62
Murray, Kevin, 146, 147
Nerenberg, Mark, 86
Nguyen, Tom, 141
Nightengale, Bob, 157
Noah, Trevor, 89
Okrent, Daniel, 61, 62,
Olsen, Elizabeth, 165
Overzet, Peter, 112, 147-149, 184, 185, 214,
Paul, Chris, 166
Payton, Walter, 128
Peppers, Bunny, 206
Perez, Stacy, 201, 202
Porter, Jontay, 119
Pratt, Chris, 165
Presley, Elvis, 81
Pullman, Jack, 70
Quintanilla, Carl, 89, 90
Rajguru, Siddherdh, 178, 179
Reynolds, Ryan, 161
Rhodes, Lindsay, 199

Ritchie, Ian, 114
Robins, Jason, 85, 86, 88, 89, 95
Romo, Tony, 153
Ross, George, 50, 56
Rudd, Paul, 164, 165
Russo, Joe, 165
Samuel, Deebo, 106
Santini, Albert, 59
Saux, Stephen, 163
Schefter, Adam, 115
Schwartz, Brian, 86, 88
Sears, Andrew, 141-143, 219
Sebring, Francis, 35, 36
Shaheed, Farid, 119, 120
Singal, Raghav, 215-218
Soda, Chet, 49
Spade, David, 168, 169
Spieth, Travis, 88, 180
St. Brown, Amon-Ra, 106
Stern, Stacie, 116, 193, 203-205
Stirling, Scotty, 50, 51, 53, 54, 55, 56, 62
Sullivan, John, 214
Swardson, Nick, 169
Swift, Taylor, 205, 206
Syken, Noah, 218
Tagliabue, Paul, 82
Taylor, Bruce, 68, 69, 77
Theismann, Joe, 17
Thorn, John, 36
Trout, Mike, 168
Tunnell, Bill, 50
Twerski, Elisha, 144
Valenzuela, Kendall, 193
Wallach, Daniel, 81, 82, 89
Waller, Darren, 157
Wasserman, Casey, 133
Wasowicz, Laura, 38
Westbrook, Brian, 99
Wilson, Rainn, 163, 165
Winkenbach, Bill, 44, 47, 50, 51, 53, 55, 62, 81, 203
Winkenbach, Gerald, 54,
Witten, Jason, 153
Wolf, Rick, 74, 75, 76, 118, 132, 160, 220
Wolf, Ron, 51
Woodford, Rachel, 198, 199
Yates, Field, 17, 136, 137
Zeidenfeld, Al, 17, 189-191

Peter Funt...

...is a television host, speaker and columnist, continuing the Funt Family tradition of making people smile.

In addition to hosting the landmark series "Candid Camera," Peter's work has appeared often in *The Wall Street Journal*, *USA Today* and *Washington Post*. His writing and public appearances contain the same pointed social observations that have made "Candid Camera" popular since its invention by Peter's dad, Allen, back in 1947.

Peter Funt made his first appearance on "Candid Camera" when he and the legendary series were each just three years old. Peter posed as a shoeshine boy who charged $10 per shoe. He has since appeared in hundreds of "Candid Camera" sequences and hosted more than 250 network episodes. Earlier in his career, Peter spent five years as a journalist with ABC News in New York.

Peter received his degree in journalism from the University of Denver. In 2010 he returned to the Denver campus to be honored as a Master Scholar in Arts and Humanities. He is a winner of the Silurian's Award for radio news reporting, for his ABC News coverage of racial disturbances in Asbury Park, N.J., and he's a recipient of the Angel Award for television.

Peter and his wife Amy reside in Central California. They have two children, Stephanie and Danny. His favorite pastimes are golf and baseball — except when he's obsessing over his fantasy football lineups.

Also by Peter Funt...

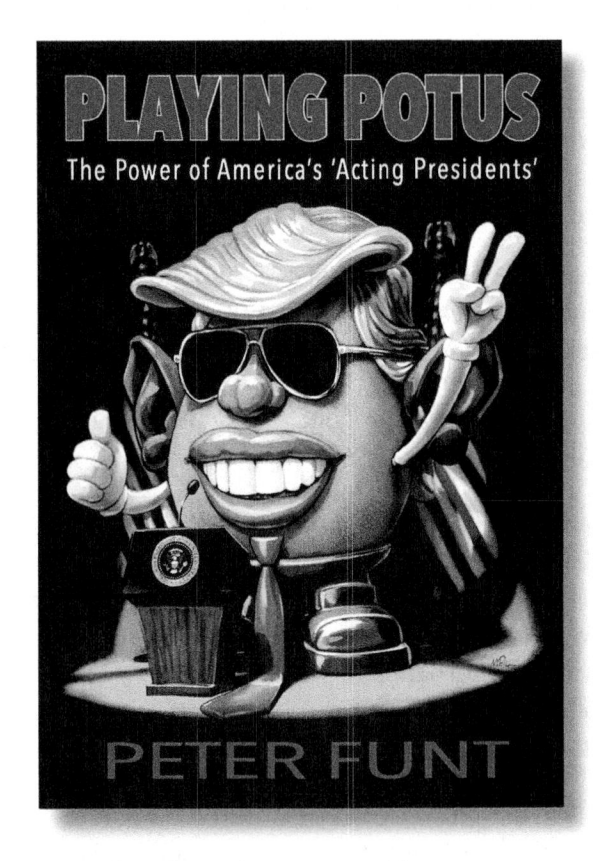

PLAYING POTUS
The Power of America's 'Acting Presidents'

PETER FUNT

Connecting the dots between those in power and those speaking schtick to power. A fun read that looks at a unique group of comedians and the challenges they faced as impersonators of U.S. presidents. Over 50 interviews provide insights from noted performers Dana Carvey, Darrell Hammond, Jay Pharoah, Rich Little, Al Franken, Harry Shearer and other presidential mimics.

"Peter Funt's collection of stories, memories and misfit adventures is insightful, hilarious, and just plain fun. I loved following Peter's journey. I'm honored to be part of it!"
—*Mayim Bialik*

In this collection of essays, Peter Funt examines our world with an eye toward major issues as well as those little things that sometimes drive us crazy.

Printed in Great Britain
by Amazon